Surveying
the Historical Books

JOSEPH M. GETTYS

* JOHN KNOX PRESS
RICHMOND, VIRGINIA

OTHER BIBLE STUDIES BY THE SAME AUTHOR

Teaching the Historical Books

Surveying the Pentateuch

Teaching the Pentateuch

How to Enjoy Studying the Bible

Teaching Pupils How to Study the Bible (Leader's Guide)

How to Teach the Bible

Teaching Others How to Teach the Bible (Leader's Guide)

How to Study Luke

How to Teach Luke

How to Study John

How to Teach John

How to Study Acts

How to Teach Acts

How to Study I Corinthians

How to Teach I Corinthians

How to Study Ephesians

How to Teach Ephesians

How to Study the Revelation

How to Teach the Revelation

LIBRARY OF CONGRESS CATALOG CARD NUMBER: 63-8701
© M. E. BRATCHER 1963
PRINTED IN THE UNITED STATES OF AMERICA
8837(20)D.4923

Dedicated to

my colleagues at

PRESBYTERIAN COLLEGE

Fellow students of truth

in a Christian context

* Contents

A Personal Word to Students

This survey of the Historical Books of the Old Testament will be as good as you make it. You may feel that too much help is given for a survey. Again, you may feel that not enough detail is dealt with in the material. We suggest that while this series is prepared in thirteen lessons to cover a quarter, they may well be divided into twenty-six lessons for two quarters. If this is done, we suggest that the first approach to each lesson be based on the daily Bible readings. This will give an over-all picture of each lesson. Then the second approach may be to use the detailed study. This has some repetition, but lifts out certain emphases which throw the whole into sharper focus. So remember this rule: Take the Bible readings the first class period on a given body of material, and the detailed study the second time. This is proposed in the back as suggestions for twenty-six lessons.

The hardest task you will have is to make time for the daily Bible readings. Discipline yourself for this and hold yourself to it. During the second week, if you are going half as fast, spend an equal amount of time each day on the detailed study and the suggested readings. They will prove doubly helpful after you have made a direct approach to the Bible itself.

Above all, remember that this study guide is designed to get you into the Bible for yourself. It uses helps constantly, but not as a substitute for studying the sacred text. The heart of this study guide is not the guide itself, but the Bible to which it points and whose pages it seeks to illuminate.

If possible, work with one or more persons to share what you have learned. Study groups are found in most churches. Organize one if necessary. Get in one and share the best thing you find week by week. May the Spirit of God guide you in this new adventure in learning!

Introduction and Joshua 1-12

OUR PURPOSE AND POINT OF VIEW

As was indicated in *Surveying the Pentateuch,* the purpose of these studies is to help students gain a better understanding of the total sweep and message of Old Testament books, not to present all the details of any given book of the Bible. This purpose places rigid limitations on dealing with many problems of interpretation. It will recognize the use of sources but will not be a critical or source-type of study.

We believe that some false assumptions regarding sources have hindered the proper interpretation of both the Old and the New Testaments. For instance, some people, particularly lay people, believe that any reference to sources is a denial of the trustworthiness of the inspiration or authority of the Bible. Some interpreters may use sources as a means of discrediting the Bible. But many reverent scholars enhance our understanding of its message by their careful research and study. We ought not to close our minds to their important work out of fear that the Bible cannot stand such study. It can and it has. We are the richer for the labors of such men.

Yet there are some further assumptions that we would call in question. One is that sources earlier in time are always more reliable than later sources. On this assumption Mark gives a more correct interpretation of the life and meaning of Christ than Luke or John does. But the hidden assumption that Mark is factual because it is earlier and Luke is less factual because it was probably written later is false. For Mark gives an *interpretation* of the life and meaning of

Jesus just as Luke does. He edits and marshals his facts just as surely as Luke does. All four of the Gospel writers proclaim a faith about Jesus Christ which, as G. Ernest Wright has written, goes back to the Old Testament. Referring to Paul's sermon recorded in Acts 13:16-41, and summarizing the main points of this sermon, Wright adds: "It will be noted that this is a typical biblical statement of faith, cast not in the form of theological abstractions, but in terms of historical events which are seen as the acts of God" (*The Interpreter's Bible*, Vol. 1, pp. 349-350, but note the whole article on pages 349-389).

B. Davie Napier holds the same general point of view concerning the sources used in the Pentateuch and the Historical Books. "If the 'later' sources are interpretative, as they are, *so are the earlier*. We do not think there is anywhere in the Bible a purely objective, detached account of sequential events" (*From Faith to Faith*, p. 108). Napier writes further: "Early and late, Israel's historians are better understood in Aristotle's definition of a poet. Aristotle's historian was a mere chronicler of sequential events; his poet was one who distilled from the chronological catalogue its essence, its universal judgment and meaning." In his *A History of Israel* and his *The Kingdom of God*, while showing himself a master in seeking historical accuracy, John Bright reflects an understanding of this fundamental truth.

We propose to emphasize the unity and purpose of these books of the Old Testament in terms of the faith of Israel and the purpose of God. Norman Snaith expressed the importance of going beyond the tendency to concentrate on literary sources in these wise words:

There are limits beyond which literary analysis cannot be pressed without doing more harm than good. Even the good order of J, E, D, and P may corrupt the scholarly world. We have been so very energetic in isolating each from the other, and even within each, in separating stratum from stratum, that we have tended to forget that there might be method even in the madness which so thoroughly dovetailed them in together. Perhaps after all that madness was divine (*The Distinctive Ideas of the Old Testament*, p. 14).

We must recognize the fact that this point of view does not eliminate many of the problems of interpretation in the Historical Books. The impossibility of synchronizing certain dates in the text, of harmonizing all double accounts, of determining in some cases which is the correct historical reference, will remain with us. So also will the problem of verifying certain numbers used in the text. At these points and at others like them we must rely heavily on the work of reverent scholars. These will be suggested as resources for further reading. It is hoped that the end result will be a more intelligent and a more deeply reverent attitude toward the message of the Old Testament and toward the God who speaks through it.

As we stated in *Surveying the Pentateuch,* the finished product which has come to us across the centuries as the Bible is more than the sum of the various parts, even if we could dissect them and separate them with confidence. The inspired writer or writers who selected, edited, and perhaps interpreted (though often different strands appear to have been put alongside each other very much as they were) the sources used were presenting the faith of Israel in terms of the acts and meaning of God. They did it out of a living situation in which God revealed Himself in actual experiences (individual and corporate) in history. The inspired mind saw and at least partially understood. Where differences of opinion are presented in the same book or in succeeding books (such as the accounts of the conquest of Canaan in Joshua 1-12 and Judges 1:1-2, 5, or different attitudes toward the establishment of the monarchy under Saul), this should indicate to us that the writers intended to show us that the whole story is not told in one story or in one point of view.

It will therefore be unfair and erroneous to criticize the text for differences or to choose between two points of view when these are presented in the text. To attempt such practice may reveal more of the reader's confusion than the writer's. It will reflect our effort to force the writer into our molds of thinking rather than placing ourselves sympathetically at his disposal. Just as we expect to be understood in the total context of our life and work, so we ought to permit the inspired writers to make their own impression in their own way. The language of Scripture is a language of faith in a living, active, redeeming, ruling, loving, and sovereign God, working out His purpose in history. While therefore we must recognize the necessity of critical study, we may also at some point deal with the finished product in the form in which it has come to us. This is the concern which marks these studies.

One further word is highly important. This is a study guide, not a commentary. Do not try to force it into a commentary mold. Its purpose is not to tell students what the writer has found in the Historical Books. It is rather to guide students in their own study of the Historical Books, which is a different thing. Follow the directions and do the suggested additional reading before you evaluate. For then you will have put yourself at the disposal of God's Spirit as you read the sacred text and the interpretative help provided for your understanding. We believe that by this means God will speak most effectively to you. If you are privileged to study in a group, the sharing process will clarify your understanding and appreciation still further. We urge that you find or make time to do the daily Bible readings and the further study. It will pay large dividends in your understanding and your Christian growth. For those who wish to engage in more than thirteen class sessions, a program of twenty-six lessons is provided on page 164 of this study guide.

THE BOOK OF JOSHUA

The book of Joshua is closely related to the first five books of the Old Testament. Because it tells the story of the conquest and settlement in Canaan, which is so focal in the covenant promises of Genesis-Deuteronomy, Joshua is sometimes grouped with these books under the title of the Hexateuch, comprising the first six books of the Bible.

Joshua is likewise closely associated with the Historical Books. In the Jewish Bible it is grouped with Judges, 1 and 2 Samuel, 1 and 2 Kings, to form the earlier prophets. Except for adding Ruth to Judges, we will follow this grouping, having previously dealt with the first five books of the Old Testament in *Surveying the Pentateuch*. We will also relate a number of Old Testament prophets to their historical background in 2 Kings, but will reserve a study of their total message for a later time.

AUTHORSHIP AND DATE OF JOSHUA

As might be expected, several different views have been presented concerning the authorship of Joshua. For instance, H. Wheeler Robinson writes in his commentary on Joshua in The New Century Bible, p. 251:

> The Book of Deuteronomy is a sermon; the Book of Joshua the preacher's illustrations collected into an appendix. It describes the Conquest and Division of the Promised Land from the standpoint of a Deuteronomic preacher, six or seven centuries after the event.

G. A. Cooke, *The Book of Joshua,* pp. 1-2, 115-116, and throughout the commentary, assigns materials to proposed sources. His work may be compared with that of Robinson in The New Century Bible.

Harper's Bible Dictionary, p. 352, gives William F. Albright credit for the view that Joshua in its present form dates from the seventh century B.C., and that some parts were written as early as the tenth century B.C., suggesting that the Deuteronomic revisions date from 550-400 B.C.

John Bright, in *The Interpreter's Bible* (Vol. 2, p. 542), proposes that "Joshua is a Deuteronomic book. Like other historical books, it is the work of a historian who edited older materials available to him and cast them in the framework of his own distinctive style and viewpoint." His detailed analysis should be studied for a fair presentation of his point of view. Basically, it is that chapters 1-12 are the work of a Deuteronomic editor, based on the earlier document known as JE; with chapters 13-21 depending more on a Deuteronomic than a Priestly (P) editor. He recognizes interpolations by a Priestly writer, but not dependence on a P document in these latter chapters.

On the other hand, H. B. Reed, writing in Herbert C. Alleman's *Old Testament Commentary,* p. 329, asserts that while the identity of the author cannot be established with certainty, there is evidence in 5:9; 6:25; 15:8; and 16:10 pointing to an early date, perhaps an eyewitness. He believes that while Joshua did not write the account of his death in 24:29-33, he might have furnished some of the other materials used in the book. He leaves the date a matter of conjecture (p. 330).

Edward J. Young, in his *An Introduction to the Old Testament,* p. 173, believes that a basis of the book was written by Joshua, but that the book in its present form, while very ancient, is not from the hand of Joshua. He suggests that an elder who had been an eye-witness to most of the events probably wrote under the guidance of the Holy Spirit.

Whichever point of view is correct concerning the human author or authors (we tend to follow John Bright in his judgment), the book of Joshua has come to us across the centuries as one of the books of the Bible through which God has spoken and through which He still speaks.

THE CHARACTER OF THE BOOK OF JOSHUA

Scholars generally have accepted Judges 1 and passages like Joshua 15:13-19, 63; 16:10; 17:11-18; and 19:47 as evidence that each of the clans attempted to hew out its own "living room" in Canaan without complete success, and they have questioned seriously the historical accuracy of Joshua 1-12. Further, they have interpreted Joshua himself as perhaps a petty tribal hero "whose exploits were magnified with the ascendancy of the Joseph tribes until he became a national hero and the successor to Moses." (See *The Interpreter's Bible,* p. 546.) H. Wheeler Robinson, in *Deuteronomy, Joshua* (The New Century Bible), pp. 251-265, gives a good summary of this older view. Recognizing the complex character of the Conquest, John Bright sets forth reasons why both Judges 1 and Joshua 1-12 should be studied more carefully. Joshua 1-12, he believes, is a more schematized story centering in Joshua as a leader. He suggests that archaeology shows destructions of some places in the thirteenth, twelfth, and eleventh centuries B.C., so different accounts do not always refer to the same destruction. While in no sense does he gloss over the historical problems, Bright calls for a much greater respect for the historical character of Joshua 1-12 than is usually given.

The book of Joshua carries forward the consciousness that the people of Israel are the covenant people of God. We found this to be the unifying and controlling idea in the Pentateuch. In the Historical Books, this idea fades in favor of the Davidic covenant, which promised (with the condition of obedience) that the seed of David would continue to sit on the throne. Yet this Sinai covenant, which is very much in the mind of many of the Hebrew prophets, comes again to the fore in the finding of the book of the Law during the reforms of Josiah in 621 B.C. Actually the Deuteronomic point of view in the Historical Books never loses sight of this covenant. Loyalty and faithfulness to God in worship and conduct bring His blessing, and disobedience in worship and conduct brings punishment. A further controlling idea is that the purpose of God, which is redemptive, is being worked out in history. History is interpreted from this point of view. We must remember this fact if we are to understand the material before us.

Many persons are troubled by the fact that the book of Joshua is a story of military conquest and settlement in a land formerly occupied by another people. This is a story of ancient times, prior to the time of Jesus Christ, and this is war, even a holy war. Across many years it became a war of destiny as well as a war for survival. The outcome, like the command to engage in it, was understood to be within the will of God. Who are we to play God and to decide what should have been done? Have we not invoked God's blessing on two world wars in recent years? Jesus Christ should win the world by love, but this victory is not yet won. We face the challenge to win it. Yet we may be aware that some of the forces against which we struggle, like the forces of evil, do not yet understand the language of love.

THE PLAN OF THESE STUDIES

After a brief introduction to each of the books, we propose to provide daily Bible readings. These are important because they encourage the student to examine carefully the sacred text itself. Then we propose to lift out a few lines of thought that help to unify and clarify the text. Next we will list a limited number of additional resources for further reading. Finally we will suggest some questions for thought and discussion. Frequently references will be made in the daily Bible readings to suggested resources because they will help to answer questions that arise in the mind of the student. It is hoped that study groups will come together to share findings and to make further explorations. Suggestions for leading such groups will be made in the leader's guide, *Teaching the Historical Books*. Again we remind the student that those who wish to do a more thorough study may wish to follow the suggestions for twenty-six lessons rather than the thirteen in which these studies are arranged. This kind of outline will be found on page 164.

THE OVER-ALL STRUCTURE OF JOSHUA

The book of Joshua falls into the following major outline:

I. THE CONQUEST OF WESTERN PALESTINE (CANAAN) (chs. 1-12).

   A. Introduction (ch. 1).
   B. Crossing the Jordan, Establishing a Beachhead (chs. 2-5).
   C. Conquest of Central Palestine (chs. 6-9).
   D. Conquest of Southern Palestine (ch. 10).
   E. Conquest of Northern Palestine (ch. 11).
   F. Summary of Conquests (ch. 12).

II. DIVISION OF THE LAND (chs. 13-21).

   A. Land Already Claimed by Tribes East of the Jordan (ch. 13).
   B. Division of the Land West of the Jordan (chs. 14-21).
      1. To Caleb (ch. 14).
      2. To Judah (ch. 15).
      3. To Ephraim and Manasseh (chs. 16-17).
      4. To Other Tribes (chs. 18-19).
      5. Cities of Refuge (ch. 20).
      6. Cities for Levites (ch. 21:1-42).
   C. Conclusion and Summary of Land Division (21:43-45).

III. LAST DAYS OF JOSHUA (chs. 22-24).

   A. Settlement of Eastern Tribes (ch. 22).
   B. Joshua's Farewell Address (ch. 23).
   C. The Covenant at Shechem (ch. 24:1-28).
   D. Burial of Joshua, Joseph, and Eleazer (ch. 24:29-33).

We will now turn our attention to chapters 1-12, and will study chapters 13-24 in the next lesson.

DAILY BIBLE READINGS

Individual study *prior to* group learning is very important. God by His Spirit speaks to the individual who puts himself at the disposal of the Bible. The individual must put himself at God's disposal in a reverent and seeking attitude by his own preparation. In addition, if group study is to be most fruitful, the best insights and discoveries taken to the group will help to make it so. Let us warn you that you will not *find* time for daily reading and study. You will have to *make* time. We always make time for the things we consider most important to us. If you mean business, you will make time. If you do not, perhaps you want to be spoon-fed and will remain a babe in spiritual understanding and experience the remainder of your life. Perhaps early in the morning, or after you have finished the day's business, or after the children have gone to school in the morning or to bed at night—there is no set time for every person to make his time. Some adults may wish to study at the same time and to pause for comparing notes. Make your schedule and keep to it.

The Bible readings suggested below assume a Sunday class. You may wish to start Sunday afternoon. If so, pencil in the change in days proposed. If your study group meets on Wednesday or some other day, do the same to make the readings fit into that schedule. Keep up your reading each day and do not let it pile up on you.

MONDAY

Read Joshua 1 and 2 prayerfully. Observe the commission given to Joshua in 1:1-9. What command is given in verses 10-11? What challenge was given to the Reubenites, the Gadites, and the half-tribe of Manasseh? Note their promise and their charge to Joshua. Examine the interesting and exciting story of the spies and Rahab. How were they saved by Rahab? What was their report to Joshua?

It will frequently be helpful to read the additional resources listed at the end of each lesson as one proceeds in study. We will not repeat this suggestion each time, but believe it will be helpful.

TUESDAY

Read chapters 3-5. Observe the preparation made for passing over the Jordan. How was the covenant tied in with plans for crossing the Jordan? Note Joshua's place as the leader of this movement. How and where did the people pass over the Jordan? How was this experience commemorated by the twelve tribes? Note the teaching which was to follow. Observe the details of the crossing, the place of encampment, the order of crossing, the stones from the Jordan, the Passover feast, and the worship which followed this important crossing. Think through what these chapters say to you.

WEDNESDAY

Read chapters 6 and 7. Actually chapters 6-9 describe the conquest of the central portion of Palestine, but we are dividing these chapters for reading. A map like that on Plate IV, back of *Harper's Bible Dictionary* or *The Westminster Dictionary of the Bible,* or Plate VI, p. 42 of *The Westminster Historical Atlas* is very helpful in reading these chapters. Wise students always use maps in locating places mentioned. As you read chapters 6 and 7, observe the plan given by the Lord for the conquest of Jericho, including the plan for the seventh day. According to 6:18, from what were the Israelites to refrain? What was the result of the obedience of the people at Jericho? Who broke faith concerning the devoted things? The *hérem,* or devotion to destruction at the command of God, was considered very sacred. What was the result of Achan's sin? How was he detected and punished? Note the term used to describe this valley.

THURSDAY

Read chapters 8 and 9. What was the plan of battle at Ai? How did it work? How was the covenant renewed at Mt. Ebal? Consult commentaries concerning the story in 8:30-35 and its location here. The connection seems to be logical in reporting that the command given in Deuteronomy 11:29-30; 27:2-8, 11-14, was carried out as soon as possible. What was the strategy of the Gibeonites and how did it work? Locate Gibeon on a map. What did the Israelites do after the deception was discovered?

FRIDAY

Read chapters 10 and 11. Observe the account of the battles with the kings of the south in chapter 10. If available, note John

Bright's comment on 10:12-13 in *The Interpreter's Bible,* Vol. 2, p. 605. Trace the conquest on a map, locating the cities mentioned. How is this conquest summarized in 10:40-43? Note the places in the north mentioned in chapter 11. How is the conquest of the north described? Note the summary in verses 16-23, and particularly the statement in verse 18. This conquest was actually a long, drawn-out affair.

SATURDAY

Read chapter 12. Locate the places mentioned in this chapter. Note the total number of city-kings captured. What is your total impression of the conquest of Canaan (Palestine) given in these chapters? Keep your mind open for further light.

SUNDAY

Review chapters 1-12. Think through the story of Joshua in chapters 1-12. How was Joshua prepared for the conquest? How were the people of Israel prepared? What lessons in obedience were taught? How? What was the result of the conquest as described in chapters 1-12? Keep in mind the fact that it is not complete. What do these chapters say to you?

DETAILED STUDY

Although some scholars have questioned the trustworthiness of the picture in Joshua 1-12, the readings suggested at the end of this lesson will indicate that "there was a campaign of great violence and success during the thirteenth century" (*The Westminster Historical Atlas,* revised edition, p. 39). This campaign sought to destroy the existing city-state system, particularly in the hill country, but it was a long time before the land was completely conquered. This does not deny the possibility or the probability that persons of Hebrew background and/or faith were already settled in central Palestine in and around Shechem. In fact, the book of Genesis suggests that Shechem and Hebron may well have become centers for the seed of Abraham. The book of Joshua, which is now our concern, presents Joshua the man not merely as an Ephraimite leader who was later glorified as a leader of all Israel, but as the leader of all Israel who led a campaign of great violence and success against the Canaanite city-state system, particularly in the hill country of

Palestine. We do not claim, nor does the book of Joshua, that this was a complete conquest. But we do propose now to see how the inspired writer, usually referred to as a Deuteronomic writer (or writers), interprets this conquest with Joshua as its key figure. Further reading will help the student to become better acquainted with the historical and interpretive problems involved. We will lift out the message of Joshua 1-12 under Joshua's commission, his strategy, and his loyalty to the covenant.

A. JOSHUA COMMISSIONED AS LEADER. Ch. 1.

1. Observe the command in Joshua 1:2 and the promises made to the people and to Joshua in verses 3-5. Note the timing of this experience.
2. What specific instructions are given in verses 6-9? Observe the command to be strong and courageous, and the command to obey the book of the Law. Whose presence is promised to Joshua? These verses present a divine call, a divine program, a divine requirement, and a divine promise. These are most appropriate to Joshua's commission by God as the successor to Moses and the leader of Israel.
3. How does Joshua announce the program of God to the people in verses 10-11? Observe that he is ready for action.
4. Read Numbers 32 as a background for Joshua 1:12-18. Of what did Joshua remind the tribes who settled east of the Jordan? How did they pledge their loyalty? Note that the unity of the twelve tribes is emphasized. Joshua is now prepared for the conquest, and must work out his strategy.

B. JOSHUA'S STRATEGY. Chs. 2, 6, 8-12.

In sum, the strategy of Joshua was to establish a beachhead west of the Jordan, divide the land, and conquer the south and the north after driving a wedge through the middle. Let us examine this strategy in greater detail.

1. What was the purpose of spying out Jericho in chapter 2? Observe the way in which the spies were protected by Rahab, the instructions she gave to them, their report to Joshua, and his conclusions drawn from this report.

2. Omitting for the present the material in chapters 3-5, note the promise reported in 6:1-2. Israel was now encamped on the west side of the Jordan at Gilgal. What was the order of march around Jericho? How did the order differ on the seventh day? What was the result? Note verses 17-19 on the things devoted to the Lord, and what was excepted. Observe the description of the destruction of the city in verse 21, the saving of Rahab and her family in verses 22-25, and the curse pronounced on the city in verses 26-27. How was Joshua's prestige enhanced by this victory? The meaning of the *hêrem* (devoted things) was that these things or persons were completely consecrated to the deity as a sort of sacrifice, and were irrevocably condemned for use by the people. Observe the example in chapter 7. On the fall of Jericho, see the statement and references by John Bright in *The Interpreter's Bible,* Vol. 2, p. 577.

3. Geographically Ai is in the hill country about eleven miles north of Jerusalem, and more than a mile east of Bethel. The problem of Ai and possible explanations are given in *The Interpreter's Bible,* Vol. 2, pp. 583-584. In 7:2-5, what procedure was used to determine the force needed to capture Ai? What was the result of the first effort to capture Ai? The remainder of this chapter will be studied under the covenant relationship.

4. Following the punishment of Achan and his family, what commands were given to Joshua in chapter 8? What promises were made? What strategy was used in the battle of Ai? With what result? Observe the raising of the javelin in verse 18 (cf. vs. 26) and its effect in battle. How is the destruction of Ai described? Note that the cattle and the spoil are excluded from the *hêrem,* or devoted things. This marks the conquest of a key city in the hill country of central Palestine. In another approach we will examine 8:30-35.

5. According to chapter 9, what was the strategy of the Gibeonites? How did they deceive the Israelites? Note their location again. What decision was reached concerning the covenant made between the Israelites and the Gibeonites? What

punishment was meted out to them? Observe that with Jericho and Ai captured, and the Gibeonites as a subject people, a wedge is driven in Canaan. However, it does not extend to the Mediterranean coast.

6. According to chapter 10, what city-kings were invited by the king of Jerusalem to join him? Against whom was their attack directed? Observe the forced march during the night from Gilgal and the way the Lord helped Joshua against these kings. Plate IV in the back of *Harper's Bible Dictionary* (also Plate IV in *The Westminster Dictionary of the Bible*) or Plate VI on p. 42 of *The Westminster Historical Atlas* will be helpful in locating places. Always use these or similar maps in locating places mentioned in the text. Hebron is south of Jerusalem, Jarmuth is southwest, Debir is south-southwest, Lachish is southwest of Jarmuth, and Eglon is further southwest. Note the flight via Beth-horon and Azekah (near Jarmuth). The location of Makkedah is uncertain. On the command to the sun to stand still, see *The Interpreter's Bible,* Vol. 2, p. 605, John Calvin's commentary on Joshua, pp. 152-155, and H. Wheeler Robinson, *Deuteronomy, Joshua,* pp. 315-316. We follow Bright in his comment here and on verse 15, which breaks the story and is out of place here.

7. How is the conquest of the kings of the south described? Observe the cities mentioned. Note the summary of the conquest in central and southern Palestine in 10:40-43. The limits of "Kadesh-barnea to Gaza" (not mentioned in conquest of cities above) and "as far as Gibeon" in central Palestine suggest the whole region from the Negeb (a desert in the south) to central Palestine, including the hill country and outlying areas. The land of Goshen is not to be understood as the land of Goshen in Egypt. Jerusalem and some other key cities are not mentioned, which suggests that the conquest, even in the hill country, was not complete.

8. Using the map again, locate the places in which the kings of the north lived, as stated in chapter 11. Hazor is north of the Sea of Galilee, Madon to the west of this sea, Shimron of uncertain location, Achshaph probably near Accho, Chin-

neroth just west of the Sea of Galilee (though the reference
may be to Naphothdor in the valley of the Jordan), Mt.
Hermon north of the Sea of Galilee, and Mizpeh is uncertain. The waters of Merom probably refer to the wadi which
flows into the Sea of Galilee. Even though some of the cities
are uncertain as to their location, it is apparent that the coalition of forces was organized in northern Palestine. How was
Joshua encouraged to go out to fight these forces? What help
did he receive? Note that he pursued his enemies. Mis-
rephoth-maim seems to be northwestward from Merom toward Tyre, with Sidon further northward, both on the
Mediterranean coast. Mizpeh may be toward Mt. Hermon,
but this is not certain. Note the central location of Hazor for
these northern forces, and the fact that it was destroyed.

9. According to 11:16-23, how is the conquest of the whole land
   summarized? Observe verse 18, which suggests a long war
   with these kings. Observe the areas mentioned, and the
   Anakim (giants) in what soon came to be known as Philistia.
   Note also the repeated statement of verse 23, indicating that
   Joshua carried out the command of God to Moses.

10. Examine again the summary of the conquest east of the
    Jordan and then west of the Jordan in chapter 12. What is
    the total number of city-kings? This is largely a repetition of
    previous chapters. One area is missing, and that is the area
    around Shechem, which will be recognized presently.

C. JOSHUA'S LOYALTY TO THE COVENANT. Chs. 3-5, 8:30-35.

The final preparation for the conquest of western Canaan
emphasizes strongly the covenant relationship between God and
His people. This is the Mosaic or Sinai covenant promised to the
seed of Abraham and established under the leadership of Moses.
The ark of the covenant, which signified the presence of God, is
referred to frequently in the account of crossing the Jordan. The
tent of meeting does not come in for attention, but this does not
mean that such a tent did not exist. The presence of God was
highly significant at this stage of Israel's life as a nation.

1. In chapter 3, what instructions were given by the officers to the

people? What did Joshua say to the people and to the priests?

2. According to 3:7-13, how was the covenant to be renewed as the people came to the brink of the Jordan? Describe the way in which Israel passed over the Jordan.

3. What new things are added in chapter 4? Note the reference to the twelve stones of the twelve tribes as a memorial to what was done for the covenant people. Gilgal means a circle of stones. Observe that the memorial at Gilgal is to God's faithfulness in fulfilling His covenant promises. Note also the number of fighting men from east of the Jordan.

4. What reaction to the crossing of the Jordan is reported in 5:1? Why were the Israelites circumcised when they came to the Land of Promise west of the Jordan? Circumcision is a sign of the covenant between God and His people, established with the seed of Abraham in Genesis 17. Of what was the Passover a sign? The Passover was associated with the deliverance of the covenant people who obeyed God by sprinkling the blood on the doorpost as reported in Exodus 12. Observe that the manna ceased at Gilgal when the people ate the grain of the land.

5. The vision of Joshua in 5:13-15 is instructive. Observe that the real commander of the hosts of Israel is the Lord and not Joshua. This is designed to underline the fact that God is acting in behalf of His people, setting the stage for the conquest which follows.

6. Study 8:30-35 carefully. H. Wheeler Robinson suggests that this passage interrupts the story in its present context and that it should be omitted or read after 11:23 (*Deuteronomy, Joshua*, p. 306). John Bright recognizes 8:30-35 as a break, and suggests: "In all likelihood vss. 30-35 ought to be viewed as parallel or supplementary to 24:1-28" (*The Interpreter's Bible,* Vol. 2, p. 595). Deuteronomy 11:29-30; 27:2-8, 11-14; and Exodus 24:3-8 should be read in this connection.

According to Deuteronomy 11:29 and 27:2-8, the Israelites had been commanded to erect an altar of large stones at Mt. Ebal when they passed over the Jordan. Note that they made a sacrifice, according to the ancient command. What place did the ark have in the story? What function did the Law have? The story appears to have been placed here to show that when Mt. Ebal became accessible to the Israelites, they obeyed the command of the Lord to His covenant people.

This passage and chapter 24 suggest to us that we must not limit our thinking about Joshua to chronology alone. There is a logic in the arrangement of this book which is not dictated by our modes of thought. It appears here that the renewal of the covenant was more important to the mind of the inspired writer than was historical sequence.

D. Lessons in Living.

1. The most important lessons in living are suggested to each student by his own study of the text. In addition to such lessons, or perhaps in repetition of them, we would suggest a few worth considering.
2. God's concern for His covenant people. The book of Joshua breathes the atmosphere of God's concern. It is not just a story of conquest, but a story of God and His people in conquest.
3. God's activity in history to accomplish His purpose. The Bible sees the events of history in terms of God's mighty acts which have meaning for all time. History is God's story. It still is if we have eyes to see that this is true.
4. The importance of obedience to God's will. Disobedience brings tragic punishment and obedience brings achievement of God's purpose.
5. The efforts to keep Israel as one people. The co-operation of the eastern and western tribes, centering in the covenant relationship, receives proper emphasis in Joshua.

SUGGESTIONS FOR FURTHER READING

A. Commentaries:

Cooke, G. A., *The Book of Joshua,* Introduction and pp. 1-114.
The Interpreter's Bible, Vol. 2, pp. 541-617.
Robinson, H. Wheeler, *Deuteronomy, Joshua* (The New Century Bible), pp. 251-329.

B. Introductory and Background Material:

Alleman and Flack, *Old Testament Commentary,* pp. 144-145.

Anderson, Bernhard W., *Understanding the Old Testament,* pp. 70-84.

Bright, John, *A History of Israel,* pp. 97-127.

Finegan, Jack, *Light from the Ancient Past,* revised edition, pp. 155-167.

Pfeiffer, Robert H., *Introduction to the Old Testament,* pp. 293-313.

The Westminster Historical Atlas to the Bible, revised edition, pp. 32-36, 39-42.

Wright, G. Ernest, *Biblical Archaeology,* pp. 69-84; abridged edition, pp. 43-52.

Note: *Surveying the Pentateuch,* pp. 11-12, gives some basic helps in Bible study. A good Bible dictionary, such as *Harper's Bible Dictionary* or *The Westminster Dictionary of the Bible,* should be among the first books purchased.

QUESTIONS FOR THOUGHT AND DISCUSSION

1. Do you think it is ever right to engage in war? In a war of conquest for living room? In a war of extermination which kills innocent women and children? In what sense do you think God commanded the Israelites to conquer the land of Canaan?

2. In answer to the above questions, what is the point of view of the book of Joshua? Do you think the Israelites were wrong or right? Why? In what sense do we live in a struggle for survival?

3. Has our view of God "gone soft" so that we lose sight of His eternal justice? Do we hold ourselves as well as the Israelites to a strict interpretation of Jesus' spirit of self-sacrifice? Be honest and specific with examples.

4. Do you agree or disagree with John Bright that there was a conquest in the middle of the thirteenth century which broke the back of united opposition to the conquest of Palestine by the Israelites? Why or why not?

5. Why do you think Joshua 1-12 emphasizes the covenant relationship? Why is this relationship important for us?

6. What are the lessons you learn from Joshua for daily living?

Division and Settlement in Canaan

In the preceding lesson we observed that the hill country was weakened to a point where most of the city-state areas were no longer a threat to Israel. The major emphasis in the remainder of the book is on the division of the land by tribes. This part of the book should be read with a map of Palestine at hand. We will mention several sources, one of which may be available. Plate IV in the back of *Harper's Bible Dictionary,* or *The Westminster Dictionary of the Bible,* or John Bright's *A History of Israel;* Plate VI on page 42 of *The Westminster Historical Atlas;* or the map on page 618 of *The Interpreter's Bible,* Vol. 2, or on page 276 of G. Ernest Wright's *Biblical Archaeology* will serve the student well.

Those who use commentaries will discover two or more theories about the material of these chapters. H. Wheeler Robinson, for instance, assigns the material of these chapters chiefly to P, and calls attention to the fact that the boundaries for the tribes west of the Jordan (Numbers 34:1-15) "agree substantially with those of the land allotted by Ezekiel for the twelve tribes, on their restoration from exile (Ezek. lxvii:13-20)" (*Deuteronomy, Joshua,* p. 329). John Bright in *The Interpreter's Bible,* Vol. 2, pp. 543-546 and in the critical notes throughout the exegesis, presents the view that the basic materials in the present book were written by a Deuteronomic editor, with occasional interpolations and glosses by P. Concerning the border lists in chapters 13-19, he writes: "These border lists were based no doubt upon the actual holdings of the tribes (plus territory claimed in theory) in earliest times. They could hardly have arisen after Solomon reorganized the state along territorial lines" (p. 544). He believes that chapter 24 was probably added to an earlier version of Joshua with Deuteronomic editing (p. 545). We would agree with Bright. We remind the student that we regard this book as inspired in the form in which it has come to us.

We would suggest that these chapters may be divided into three divisions:

A. Land Already Claimed by Tribes East of the Jordan (ch. 13).
B. Division of the Land West of the Jordan (chs. 14-21).
C. Last Days of Joshua (chs. 22-24).

The student is reminded of a slightly different division on page 15 above, with more details given. Each student should work out his own basic outline of the materials. These are merely suggestive. Again we suggest that the daily Bible reading be done with a map, and with pencil and paper in hand.

DAILY BIBLE READINGS

MONDAY

Read Joshua 13-15. Observe 13:1, which states that much land is yet to be possessed. Compare 13:13. Locate the boundaries of the land allotted to the tribes mentioned in this chapter. Observe the story of Caleb's allotment in chapter 14 and that of other tribes in chapter 15. Use your map to locate boundaries. Note the reference to time in 14:10, from which approximately seven years may be suggested for the conquest of chapters 1-12, allowing thirty-eight years for the wilderness wanderings. Note 15:63.

TUESDAY

Read chapters 16-19. Observe the land division in chapters 16 and 17. What plan was followed in dividing the land among other tribes in chapter 18? Where was Joshua settled? Compare 19:51 with 14:1-2. Note the repeated idea in 13:1, 13; 15:63; and 18:3.

WEDNESDAY

Read chapters 20 and 21. Where were the cities of refuge? What was their function? Compare Numbers 35:6-34; Deuteronomy 4:41-43; 19:1-13. According to chapter 21, what cities were allotted to the Levites? Compare Numbers 35:1-8 and 1 Chronicles 6:48-51.

Note the summaries in Joshua 21:41-42 and 43-45. These latter verses may reflect a later point of view.

Thursday

Read chapter 22. Examine the evidences of the effort to maintain the solidarity of the covenant people. From what religious center did the tribes east of the Jordan depart? How was their worship at the Jordan misinterpreted? What does this story illustrate?

Friday

Read chapter 23. Observe the setting of this chapter. How does Joshua regard the things God has done through his leadership? What instructions did he give to Israel? What choice did he propose? What promises did he make?

Saturday

Read chapter 24. Note the setting of this story. Compare Joshua 8:30-35. How does Joshua summarize God's mighty acts in behalf of Israel? Note the choice proposed in verse 15, and the response in 16-18. How was the covenant here sealed? Note the three important persons whose burial is reported. Compare Genesis 50: 24-25 and Exodus 13:19.

Sunday

Review chapters 13-24. Think through these chapters and the things that stand out in your mind at this point in your study. What means most to you in your reading of Joshua 13-24? What does God say to you in your reading?

DETAILED STUDY

In this part of our study we propose to underscore the incompleteness of the conquest of Canaan, the different methods of dividing the land, and Joshua's final teaching, primarily concerning the covenant relation between God and His people.

A. The Incompleteness of the Conquest of Canaan.

It has been assumed by some scholars that the book of Joshua presents the view that the conquest of Canaan (Palestine) was complete. Let us examine further evidence that this was not true.

1. Examine 13:1-7 carefully. Note verse 1, which states a reason

for the division of the land then. What was this reason? Observe the more specific instruction in verse 7. Use a map to identify the areas listed as not yet conquered in verses 2-6. Descriptive identifications in *The Interpreter's Bible,* Vol. 2, pp. 619-620, are helpful.

2. What other group was unconquered, according to 13:13? These seem to be Aramaean states east and northeast of the Sea of Galilee. Bright suggests that the Geshurites of vs. 2b are not the same as those of verse 13, but of 1 Samuel 27:8, which appears to be in or near the area assigned to Judah.

3. Examine 14:12 in the larger context of 14:6-15. Note that Caleb who claims his territory recognizes his need of God's help in driving out the Anakim (giants) from the fortified cities. In this connection observe 15:13-19, where some of Caleb's (and Othniel's) conquests are noted.

4. Note the reference to Jerusalem in 15:63, and compare 2 Samuel 5:6-10.

5. Compare 16:10 and 18:3. Compare also the statements about forced labor in 1 Kings 9:21 and Joshua 17:12-13, and note the groups involved in each case.

6. What command was given the tribes of Ephraim and Manasseh in 17:14-18? The barren slopes of Palestine today witness to the clearing of the land.

7. Examine Joshua 23:1-5. What has been accomplished through Joshua? What yet remains to be done?

   These references verify Bright's insistence that Joshua 1-12 presents a schematized account of the conquest which broke resistance in the hill country, leaving much to be done by tribal and individual action.

B. METHODS OF DIVIDING THE LAND.

1. Compare Joshua 13:8-33 and Numbers 32. This is a repetition of a division made under Moses.

2. How does Caleb's request in Joshua 14:6-15 refer to his part in spying out the land? The references to Caleb's age as forty in the wilderness and eighty-five now (deducting thirty-eight for

the wilderness wanderings) again suggest approximately seven years for the conquest of Canaan.

3. Examine the account of the allotment in 14:1-6. Observe that Judah, Ephraim, and Manasseh are dealt with in chapters 14-17, and that Gilgal is the geographical center. Concerning probable sources and editorial revisions of these chapters, see John Bright, *The Interpreter's Bible,* Vol. 2, pp. 542-545, 624, 630, 633-636, 639.

4. Observe the center in Shiloh in chapter 18. Note the question in verse 3. What instructions were given to the tribes? Observe the omission of the tribes beyond the Jordan in this report.

5. The gift of land to Joshua has been recognized in 19:45-50. Note the summary in 19:51 and compare the introduction in 18:1.

Students should see H. Wheeler Robinson, *Deuteronomy, Joshua* (The New Century Bible), p. 329, and John Bright, *The Interpreter's Bible,* pp. 544-545, for a study of the similarities of the boundaries in Joshua, in Numbers 34:1-15, and in Ezekiel 47-48. The allotment in Joshua is regarded as God's will for the covenant people.

6. According to chapter 20, how were the cities of refuge assigned? For what purpose? Compare Numbers 35:6, 9-34, and Deuteronomy 19:1-13, 4:41-43, with this chapter.

7. How were the Levites assigned to cities and pasture lands in chapter 21? Observe the assignment by families, according to the command of the Lord through Moses.

The methods used to divide the land suggest division according to the plan of God, that Joshua and Caleb were given land for meritorious service, and that lots were used as a part of the division. It appears that some kind of search preceded the division of much of the land, and that in some cases, at least, a religious ceremony was associated with the division.

C. Joshua's Final Teaching and Death.

1. In chapter 22, how were the tribes east of the Jordan commended by Joshua? What instructions were given to them?

With what did they return home from Shiloh?

2. According to verses 16-20, what charge was brought against these tribes for worshipping at the Jordan? What was their reply in verses 21-29? Note how they pledged their solidarity as the people of God.

3. Examine again the things God has done, the things against which the Israelites are warned, and the requirements laid upon them. Compare Deuteronomy 26-28 for the blessings and cursings upon them.

4. Study the additional account of Joshua's farewell to the people at Shechem in chapter 24. Observe the summary of history in verses 1-13. Compare Numbers 33 and Deuteronomy 1:1— 4:40. The finger of God is evident in the history of Israel.

Several problems of interpretation are considered in *The Interpreter's Bible,* Vol. 2, p. 667; Bernard Anderson, *Understanding the Old Testament,* p. 87; and John Bright, *A History of Israel,* pp. 142-151. The Septuagint Version (a Greek translation of the Old Testament completed about 150 B.C.) places the covenant ceremony at Shiloh instead of Shechem. The other question is whether the covenant at Shechem involved relatives of the Hebrews who did not go to Egypt. Whatever the answers to these questions, it appears that chapter 24 is used to bring the book of Joshua to a grand climax with a challenge to all Israel to remain in covenant relationship with God.

5. What is the challenge and the choice before Israel in verses 14-15? How do the people reply? Examine verses 19-20, 21, 22-23, and 24 for the dialogue between Joshua and the people. In what two ways did Joshua seal the covenant between God and His people in verses 25-28? Note what he did afterwards.

It is clear that Joshua was greatly concerned that Israel remain faithful and loyal to God as the covenant people. Surely a renewed faith and a willing obedience will draw us closer to God in a world threatened with extinction. The love of God in Jesus Christ constrains us to obey in faith, to serve with resolution, to live with dynamic power, and to give ourselves to God's will with determined purpose.

D. Lessons in Living.

1. The best lessons in living are always those determined by the student himself. We make some suggestions each time to stimulate thinking.

2. The concern of God for the settlement and peace of His people after they had broken the back of united resistance in the hill country of Palestine.

3. The importance of leadership in the nation. Whether Joshua's leadership has been played up or not, this point is made very clearly. No nation moves forward without dedicated and capable leaders.

4. The importance of the covenant relationship for all Israel. Whether the covenant was with the descendants of the twelve tribes only, or included others in the larger family of Israel, the people were to be one people under God in Palestine.

5. The challenge to faithfulness for all the Israel of God. The way of willing obedience is still with us as it was with Israel.

SUGGESTIONS FOR FURTHER READING

A. Commentaries:

Cooke, G. A., *The Book of Joshua* (Cambridge Bible), pp. 115-224.
The Interpreter's Bible, Vol. 2, pp. 541-549, 617-673.
Robinson, H. Wheeler, *Deuteronomy, Joshua* (The New Century Bible), pp. 329-385.

B. Introductory and Background Material:

Albright, William F., *From the Stone Age to Christianity,* pp. 254-272.
Anderson, Bernhard W., *Understanding the Old Testament,* pp. 84-91.
Bright, John, *A History of Israel,* pp. 117-151.
The Westminster Historical Atlas to the Bible, revised edition, pp. 39-42.
Young, Edward J., *An Introduction to the Old Testament,* pp. 170-178.

QUESTIONS FOR THOUGHT AND DISCUSSION

1. What right, if any, did Joshua have to divide the land of Canaan, better known to us as Palestine, among the tribes of Israel? In what sense was this the will of God as reflected in Joshua 13-24?

2. Why was it important for the twelve tribes to achieve unity and solidarity even before the period of the kings under Saul and David? Further illustrations will appear in our study of Judges.

3. What difference, if any, is made in considering the Joseph tribes (and perhaps the tribe of Judah) in chapters 14-17 as tribes which had settled prior to the invasion of Canaan under Joshua? Is this the point of view of the book of Joshua? Of other Old Testament books? Investigation of this question will be more profitable for those with advanced training.
4. Why is the covenant relationship between God and Israel given continued emphasis in the book of Joshua? Why is this relationship equally important for us?
5. What does the book of Joshua say to us about our personal problems? Our national and international problems? Are Communist leaders right in proposing that the future belongs to them because they are determined to make it so, and because history is on their side? What is our mission? How important is one's mission in achieving a goal? Does our nation have a mission? What is it?

Judges and Deliverers in Israel

The book of Judges deals with the period of Israel's history which follows the conquest and division of the land described in Joshua. As our study of Joshua indicated, this conquest was by no means complete. This fact is underscored heavily in Judges 1:1—2:5, which gives a briefer but in some senses a parallel account of the conquest. The central theme of Judges is set forth in 2:6-23, and may be described in a cycle of history:

1. The people of Israel sin against God and worship the Baals and Ashtaroth.
2. Their enemies (without and within their boundaries) oppress them.
3. The people repent and cry for help.
4. God raises up a deliverer or judge and delivers them from their enemies.
5. After the judge dies, the people return to their sinfulness and repeat the cycle.

This theme is illustrated in chapters 3-16. Chapters 17-21 deal with the relocation of the Danites, the offense of Gibeah and its consequences, particularly to the Benjaminites. Some scholars propose 21:25 as a key verse of this book.

The title of the book comes from the Septuagint Version, which is a Greek translation from the Hebrew begun about 250 B.C. and completed approximately a hundred years later. The Greek word used to describe the book is *kritai,* meaning *judges.* The Latin Vulgate carried this same title, and it has come into general usage. A judge was primarily a deliverer who also served in some cases as a judge.

DATE, AUTHORSHIP, AND SOURCES

Not even the more conservative scholars accept the view stated in the Jewish Talmud that "Samuel wrote the book which bears his name, and the books of Judges and Ruth." Edward J. Young, among the most conservative of scholars, examines the evidence for the date of Judges in Old Testament references to events (Judges 1:21 coming prior to 2 Samuel 5:6 ff.; 1:29 prior to 1 Kings 9:16; Isaiah 9 refers to Judges 4, 5, 6; passages such as 17:6; 18:1; and 21:25 seem to imply a time early in the monarchy) and concludes that "the book was compiled during the early days of the monarchy, either under the reign of Saul or the early days of David" (*An Introduction to the Old Testament,* p. 180). While rejecting what he calls the scheme of compilation proposed by divisive criticism, he indicates that it is quite possible "that this author made use of sources, both oral and written" without destroying the literary unity of the book.

While almost all critical scholars agree that the song of Deborah in Judges 5 (and perhaps Jotham's fable in 8:8-15) is very early, going back at least to the twelfth century, they believe the present book came into existence through several stages. Jacob Myers (*The Interpreter's Bible,* Vol. 2, pp. 681-682) follows the general presentation by G. A. Cooke in the Cambridge Bible series on Judges and G. W. Thatcher in *Judges, Ruth* (The New Century Bible), in suggesting the following stages of composition:

1. Oral narrative poems composed near the time of events described in the twelfth to tenth centuries B.C.
2. Written stories in prose, possibly by the same writers responsible for the earliest documents of the Pentateuch—tenth to eighth centuries.
3. The first book of Judges composed by a combination of the oral

and written sources, probably by the person who brought together JE—eighth to seventh centuries.

4. The Deuteronomic book of Judges, consisting of the major portion of 2:6—16:31, excepting minor judges (Tola in 10:1-2, Jair in 10:3-5, Ibzan in 12:8-10, Elon in 12:11-12, and Abdon in 12:13-15, with Shamgar in 3:31 added in the late seventh century).

5. The final edition with the appendixes in 17-21, and the introduction in 1:2—2:5, with the exceptions noted in 4 above added after the Exile to form the present book of Judges. (Variations are proposed in George Foote Moore's introduction to his commentary on Judges-Ruth in the I.C.C., pp. xix-xxxv.) Eric Rust in the Layman's Bible Commentary follows the same general pattern proposed by Myers.

THE CHRONOLOGY OF JUDGES

If we examine the years of oppression, we will find that they varied in length. If we examine the periods of rest in between oppressions, we find that they fall into periods of twenty, forty, and eighty years after the major judges of Israel. See, for instance, 3:11, 30; 5:31; 8:28; 16:31. Again, if the periods of oppression and of rest or judging are added together, the total will be 410 years. However, when we recognize that not even in the case of Deborah and Barak were all of the tribes engaged in action against Israel's enemies, and in many cases only one tribe was so engaged, we must be careful about adding all of these together.

The beginning of David's reign over Judah is now pretty generally fixed at approximately 1000 B.C. This would make the beginning of Saul's reign about 1020 B.C. The major thrust of the Israelites in Palestine would be between 1250 and 1020 B.C., which is the period (beginning about 1250) shown by archaeological findings to have been the period of conquest for many of the major cities of Palestine. The Philistines came to Palestine about or soon after 1200 B.C., and this must also be taken into account in fixing dates. The problems of chronology are treated helpfully in John Bright, *A History of Israel*, pp. 151-160; G. Ernest Wright, *Biblical Archaeology*, pp. 85-97; abridged edition, pp. 55-65; *The Westminster Historical Atlas to the Bible*, pp. 15, 43-46.

THE OVER-ALL STRUCTURE

The present book of Judges may be outlined as follows:

A. REVIEW AND INTERPRETATION OF CONQUEST (1:1—2:5).

B. THE JUDGES OF ISRAEL (2:6—16:31).

1. Introduction to the story of the judges (2:6—3:6).
2. Othniel versus Cushan-rishathaim of Mesopotamia (3:7-11).
3. Ehud versus Eglon of Moab (3:12-30).
4. Shamgar versus the Philistines (3:31).
5. Deborah and Barak versus Jabin of Canaan (and Sisera his general) (chs. 4-5).
6. Gideon versus the Midianites (chs. 6-8).
7. Abimelech versus Jotham and the men of Shechem (civil strife within Israel) (ch. 9).
8. Tola (10:1-2).
9. Jair (10:3-5).
10. Jephthah versus the Ammonites (10:6—12:7).
11. Ibzan (12:8-10).
12. Elon (12:11-12).
13. Abdon (12:13-15).
14. Samson versus the Philistines (chs. 13-16).

C. APPENDIXES (chs. 17-21).

1. Micah and the Danites (chs. 17-18).
2. The Levite and his concubine (ch. 19).
3. Israel punishes Gibeah in Benjamin (ch. 20).
4. Wives provided for the Benjaminites (ch. 21).

DAILY BIBLE READINGS

MONDAY

Read Judges 1:1—3:6, noting the division at 2:5. As you read, observe the tribes that went against the Canaanites in the south, the reference to Othniel and Caleb, the reference to Jerusalem in 1:8, 21, the cycle of history presented, and the incomplete conquest of the land west of the Jordan. Observe also what is said about

Ephraim and Manasseh, the sons of Joseph. Keep a map before you, and note the further reading proposed at the end of each lesson.

TUESDAY

Read chapters 3:7—5:31. Examine the account of the oppressions and deliverances in these chapters. Note the major deliverances from the Moabites to the south and the Canaanites to the north, the leaders involved, and the tribes who assisted Deborah and Barak.

Let us say a word about the Baals and Asheroth (Astarte, Ashtoreth, and sometimes the plural, Ashtatoth) because these designations for Canaanite gods are used so frequently in Judges. The chief Baal, or god, was named El, or Hadad in the 15th and 14th centuries B.C., and sometimes Zabul (the Exalted), and Lord of heaven. Baal's wife was named Asherah. She is supposed to have borne him many gods and goddesses. In Canaanitish worship she is associated with fertility. The chief storm god, the Phoenician Baal, somehow imparted his character to the Baals, or Baal of Canaan, whose wife, Anath, was the goddess of love and war. As the Baal sent rains and hence fruit for the ground, so the Ashtoreth sent sexual fertility, the fruit of the womb. The gods and goddesses are not clearly defined, but the plural becomes singular in Palestine, perhaps in part to compete with the one God of the people of Israel. G. Ernest Wright, *Biblical Archaeology,* pp. 106-116, and John Bright, *A History of Israel,* pp. 137-142, are among the resources which give an excellent summary of the Canaanitish and Israelitish views of their gods.

WEDNESDAY

Read chapters 6-8. The Midianites were nomadic tribes from the Arabian desert, and were traditionally related to Abraham but not to Isaac. (See Genesis 25:1-6.) Observe in this story, which may have brought together more than one strand of tradition, the call of Gideon, the means of confirmation, the reduction of his army, and his smashing victory. Observe what happened in Israel at Gideon's death.

THURSDAY

Read chapters 9 and 10. What were Abimelech's ambitions, and how was he reproved by Jotham? Observe his military exploits, and the way Abimelech met his death. What new elements appear in the cycle of history in chapter 10?

FRIDAY

Read chapters 11 and 12 carefully. Who was Jephthah? What bargain did he make with the men of Gilead? Why? Note the dialogue between Jephthah and the king of the Ammonites, Jephthah's vow, and its consequences. Observe also the war against the Ephraimites.

The vow was a Jewish act of devotion and was probably a human sacrifice like that required by Chemosh the god of the Ammonites. Another view is that it was the devotion of his daughter as a virgin priestess at a local shrine. We favor the former view. The carrying through of this vow indicates both the integrity of Jephthah in holding to his rash vow and the courage of his daughter in giving her life to preserve her father's integrity.

SATURDAY

Read chapters 13-16. Observe how Samson was set apart at his birth, how he got into serious trouble with the Philistines, how God delivered him, how he finally yielded to the wiles of Delilah and was captured, and how he killed more Philistines at his death than he had during his lifetime.

SUNDAY

Review chapters 1-16. Get clearly fixed in mind the brief description of the conquest of Canaan in 1:1—2:5, the introduction to the cycle of history in 2:6—3:6, and the series of examples given in the remainder of these chapters. You may wish to chart the major oppressions and deliverances, noting the place of the minor judges in the story. Consider also the places mentioned, and the lessons in living that these chapters teach. Keep alert for things you may wish to explore in your further study.

DETAILED STUDY

We propose to examine the historical account of the conquest and settlement in Canaan in 1:1—2:5, and the cycle of history which sets the pattern for the major portion of 2:6—16:31. It is obvious from the text itself and from the helps for the study of Judges that these serve as primary means of carrying forward the message of Judges.

A. THE CONQUEST AND SETTLEMENT OF CANAAN. Chs. 1:1—2:5.

By way of background we may remind ourselves of the older view of Judges stated by Thatcher in The New Century Bible, pp. 15-16: "The recognition that the conquest of Palestine was gradual, was made by the tribes separately, and was very incomplete, shows it [Judges 1:1—2:5] to be much more reliable than the parallel story in Joshua, where the Hebrews are represented from a later point of view, acting as one people and accomplishing the conquest as they *should* rather than as they did." On the other hand, more recent scholars like John Bright, supported by strong archaeological evidence, give much greater credence to the account in Joshua of a major thrust by a combined force under Joshua in the hill country before the more complete settlement by tribes in the territory allotted to them. (See *The Interpreter's Bible,* Vol. 2, pp. 546-548; *A History of Israel,* pp. 118-120; and other resources suggested at the end of this lesson.) We understand the books of Joshua and Judges to present this latter point of view, each written and to be understood in the light of its own purpose and message.

1. Remembering the major thrust under Joshua described in Joshua 10-12, the division of the land in Joshua 13-19, and the efforts at achieving unity in Joshua 23 and 24, note the tribes assigned to fight in the south. Who were these tribes, and against what kings or cities did they fight? Use a map to follow the account of the conquest. The book of Joshua suggests seven years for the major thrust, the first part of which was in the south (following the driving of the wedge in the middle of Palestine). Judges 1 may describe a second conquest.

2. Who assisted the tribe of Judah in the conquest of the south, according to 1:16-20? What area were the men of Judah unable to take? Why? Note that the Benjaminites were not able to keep Jerusalem, even if they did win a battle against the city. (Compare 1:8 and 21.)

3. What chief city was conquered by the house of Joseph in

verses 22-26? (Compare Genesis 28:19; 35:6; 48:3; Joshua 18:13 for references to Bethel as Luz.) G. Ernest Wright in his *Biblical Archaeology,* p. 87, tells us that the excavation of 1934 at Bethel in which he participated shows no fewer than four destructions of Bethel by fire in the 12th and 11th centuries B.C., which was the period of time covered in the book of Judges. This account in Judges 1:22-26 is probably one such conquest of the city. What further conquests by Ephraim and Manasseh are recorded in verses 27-29? Observe that this was not a complete conquest.

4. What repeated expression is used to describe the failure of the tribes of Zebulun, Asher, and Naphtali in verses 31-33? How were the Danites "bottled up" to the hill country in their area? By whom? The word Amorites means "westerners," but these were probably Canaanites.

5. In 2:1-5, it is stated that the Israelites were led from Gilgal to Bochim, which has not been located, but which may be in or near Bethel. How was the covenant renewed here? What commands had the covenant people failed to obey? What did the people do when they were reminded of their failure? The term Bochim means "weeping." Note that the people sacrificed to God, perhaps seeking forgiveness.

This introduction bespeaks an incomplete conquest of the land allotted to the nine and a half tribes west of the Jordan. The early glow and purpose gave way to acceptance of Canaanite ways, customs, and worship. Such acceptance proved to be a great trial to Israel. This was contrary to the requirements placed on the covenant people. The people appear to be willing to weep over their failure, but lacked the driving power necessary to complete the conquest of the areas allotted to them. The remainder of the book of Judges is built on this failure in terms of the cycle of history already outlined. To that cycle of history let us now turn our attention.

B. THE CYCLE OF HISTORY IN JUDGES 2:6—16:31.

1. How are the death and burial of Joshua described in 2:6-10?

Compare with Joshua 24:28-31. Observe Joshua's reported age at the time of his death. Observe also the statement in Judges 2:10 concerning the new generation which did not know firsthand the work God had done for their fathers.

2. What is the main point of Judges 2:11-13? This is the first stage in the cycle of history. Note the next stage in verses 14 and 15. Usually there was a cry for help or a confession of sin following a period of oppression. Note the next stage in verse 16. The final stage is presented in verse 17. What is it? The period of rest usually is given at 20, 40, or 80 years.

3. How does the consciousness of the covenant relation between God and His people appear in verses 18-23? Note especially verses 20-23 in this context. Disobedience to God brought failure, and the people of Canaan remained as a test of obedience for the people of God. Observe how this concept is carried over into 3:1-6. What nations are mentioned as a test for Israel's obedience? What did the Israelites do as they lived in Canaan? What does their experience say to us concerning loyalty to God and obedience to His commands?

4. Judges 3:7-11 states the experience of Israel with a concrete example, using Othniel as the first judge. Observe the worship of false gods, the oppression of the king of Mesopotamia for 8 years, the cry for help, the judge who delivered, and the 40 years of rest that followed. Othniel was apparently a nephew of Caleb and was associated with the tribe of Judah.

5. Who was the oppressor (or who were the oppressors) in the second cycle in 3:12-30? For how long did the oppression last? The Amalekites were desert tribes, and the Ammonites lived east of the Jordan. The city of palms was probably Jericho. You have already read the story of Ehud, but note in this reading the number of Moabites who were killed and the long period of rest that followed.

We ordinarily suppose that each of these oppressions followed the period of rest reported. Some of the oppressions of different areas by different kings may have been more or less simultaneous. The references proposed under the consideration of chronology above should be consulted in this connection.

6. Observe that Jabin, the king of Canaan, whose capital was Hazor in the north, was the oppressor from whom Deborah and Barak delivered Israel in chapters 4-5. Study Deborah's unusual leadership and the story of Sisera and Jael, who was the wife of Heber the Kenite. Observe the summary in 4:23-24 and the song in chapter 5. This is believed to be a very ancient song. Note what it says about the different tribes and their response or lack of response to Deborah's call for help.

7. We will not attempt to deal with all the details of Gideon's story in chapters 6-8, but will point to some significant facts. Observe who the oppressors of the Israelites were for 7 years, as stated in 6:1-2. These were desert tribesmen who lived beyond Moab and Edom in the Arabian desert. By what means did the Midianites (and Amalekites) make life miserable for the people of Israel? It is interesting that camel raids are first mentioned here. Of what does the prophet of God remind the Israelites in 6:7-10? The requirements of the covenant are not forgotten.

8. Observe the two phases in the call of Gideon in verses 11-24 and 25-32. In the first, where was Gideon and why? How was he addressed? What was his reply? What was the angel's reply and command? How did Gideon feel about his ability? What promise was made to him? This experience is similar to that of Moses at the burning bush in Exodus 3 and 4. Observe that Gideon built an altar and worshiped God in connection with his call to service. Ophrah in Manasseh has not been definitely placed. F. M. Abel places it between Tabor and Bethshean, but this is not certain.

The second phase of Gideon's call was a call to action, and this action was to destroy the altar of Baal erected by his father, and to sacrifice a bull to God on a new altar there. Why did Gideon do this at night? What happened as a consequence the next morning? Note the reaction of his father. From what tribes did Gideon receive help against the Midianites?

9. By what signs was Gideon encouraged to go against the Midianites? How was the army of Israel trimmed to 300? What was the strategy against the Midianites and how did it work? Observe the battle cry. What two princes were killed by the men of Ephraim? Note how "touchy" the men of Ephraim were, and Gideon's tact in dealing with them. Observe how Gideon destroyed the kings of Midian. Why did Gideon refuse to rule over the people of Israel? Note how Gideon did a large disservice to his people with the spoils of victory. Observe also how Abimelech is introduced, and the things that happened in Israel after Gideon's death. Abimelech sought his own ends by civil war, and his death is regarded as a judgment from God. What does he say to us?

10. In chapter 10 observe the tribes who suffered from the Ammonite oppression. How are the Israelites reminded of the covenant obligations in 10:10-16? Observe the references to God's deliverances, and their repeated confession of sin. According to 11:1-3, who was Jephthah? What bargain did Jephthah make with the elders of Israel when they requested him to become their leader? Observe how his vow cost him dearly after God had given him the victory over the Ammonites. This has been noted in the daily Bible readings. His dealings with the men of Ephraim have also been observed.

11. Judging by the amount of space devoted to each, the major deliverances were those from Jabin the king of Canaan in the north, from Midian to the east, and from the Philistines to the southwest. The story of deliverance from the Philistines differs from the others in that it centers primarily in one man, Samson, rather than in a person who led one or more tribes in battle. According to chapter 13, how was Samson set apart from the time he was promised and born? Note verse 25 as a hint of the kind of power he is to have.

12. Chapters 14 and 15 center in Samson's experience with the woman of Timnah. Why did Samson insist on having her as his wife? Note the reason given in 14:4. How does the riddle play an important part in his slaying of thirty men? Why did Samson seek vengeance on the Philistines and his

father-in-law? How did Samson escape from the men of Judah? How many Philistines did Samson slay when they came to take him? Note also the provision of water, and the name of two places commemorating certain events. Observe the summary in 15:20. Some scholars believe chapter 16 was added to the Samson story at a later time.

13. How did Samson escape from Gaza? Examine the steps by which Delilah secured the secret of Samson's strength and took away the symbol of his Nazirite vow. Observe the comment in 16:20. Where was Samson imprisoned by the Philistines? How was his sight taken from him?

14. Observe how the power of God is set over against the power of Dagon the god of the Philistines in 16:23-31. What did Samson do to avenge the loss of his eyes? How is this playboy of Israel a means of plaguing the Philistines? Note his epitaph in 16:30b.

This series of oppressions and deliverances illustrates over and over again the fundamental thesis of Judges. Obedience in worship and conduct brings God's blessing, but disobedience brings punishment.

C. THE COVENANT RELATIONSHIP.

The covenant relationship is not given particular emphasis in Judges directly, but it does appear in several places. For instance, the statement of theme in 2:18—3:6; the song of Deborah in chapter 5; the oppression of Midian and the call of Gideon in 6:7-18; the reply of the Israelites during the Ammonite oppression in 10:10-16; the experience of Manoah and his wife who were told to set apart Samson under a Nazirite vow; the power given to Samson through this vow, emphasizing the importance of faithfulness to this vow, particularly in chapter 16—all speak eloquently concerning the covenant relationship. While the underlying message of Judges is attributed by most scholars to the Deuteronomist, we may recognize this lesson not merely because the prophetic spirits in Israel understood it, but because this is the message God would teach His people. This is therefore God's message to man, not merely that of some individual who so interpreted Israel's history. We do well to keep this distinction in mind, not only for our understanding of Israel's history, but also for our obedience to the message of God through that history.

The book of Judges therefore speaks of God in these chapters through a prophetic interpretation of history. The incomplete conquest, the schematic series of illustrations of the cycle of history set forth in 2:6—3:6, and the exploits of deliverers called judges within the framework of that history all point to the importance of obedience to God's revealed will. This is all the more remarkable as we discover evidences of a primitive struggle for survival in a land filled with enemies without and within. The struggle against the Philistines will be carried forward in the account in 1 Samuel, where it becomes more acute. But this book says that God is over and in history, even in a struggle for survival. Does not the book speak to us in our day of power struggles? How necessary it is for us, with the greater ethical light since the coming of Jesus Christ, to seek and to obey the will of God in our struggle for survival in the twentieth century!

D. LESSONS IN LIVING.

1. Perhaps you have already listed your own. We will state a few.
2. The importance of obedience to God in personal life. Samson serves as the example par excellence.
3. The importance of keeping God as Lord in national life and in international relationships. He is still Lord of history.
4. The necessity of religion as a controlling force in all ethical relationships. The rules of living are not simple and easy, but we could obey God much better than we are doing.

SUGGESTIONS FOR FURTHER READING

A. COMMENTARIES:

Cooke, G. A., *The Book of Judges* (Cambridge Bible), Introduction and pp. 1-156.

The Interpreter's Bible, Vol. 2, pp. 677-798.

Moore, George F., *A Critical and Exegetical Commentary on Judges* (I.C.C.), Introduction and pp. 1-365.

Rust, Eric C., *Judges, Ruth, I and II Samuel* (Layman's Bible Commentary, Vol. 6), pp. 7-58.

Thatcher, G. W., *Judges, Ruth* (The New Century Bible), pp. 3-141.

B. INTRODUCTORY AND BACKGROUND MATERIAL:

Anderson, Bernhard W., *Understanding the Old Testament*, pp. 81-114.
Bright, John, *A History of Israel*, pp. 151-160.
   The Kingdom of God, pp. 17-33.
Finegan, Jack, *Light from the Ancient Past*, revised edition, pp. 163-177.
Napier, B. Davie, *Song of the Vineyard*, pp. 132-145.
Pfeiffer, Robert H., *Introduction to the Old Testament*, pp. 314-337.
The Westminster Historical Atlas, revised edition, pp. 43-46.
Wright, G. Ernest, *Biblical Archaeology*, pp. 85-119; abridged edition, pp. 1-19, 53-65.
Young, Edward J., *An Introduction to the Old Testament*, pp. 179-187.

QUESTIONS FOR THOUGHT AND DISCUSSION

1. Is it possible to harmonize the accounts of the conquest of Canaan in Joshua 1-12 and Judges 1:1—2:5? If not, why not? If so, how?
2. Does God lead us into wars of survival? Why or why not? Do you think God required the Israelites to drive out completely the people of Canaan? Why do you think as you do? What are some of the long-range factors to be considered in your answer?
3. How could God use a playboy like Samson to accomplish His purpose in Israel? Could Samson have been more usable than he was? Why do you think so? Can God use us even with our imperfections? Should we strive to become more and more like our Lord as He uses us? Why? How?
4. How do you understand history? Is there such a thing as history, per se? How do we measure interpretations of history? Do you believe that God is Lord of history? In what sense? Why do you think as you do?
5. What responsibility for making history does our Lord give to us as a nation today? How may we discharge our responsibility? In what sense is our search for His will in all things and our living witness to our faith a part of this responsibility?
6. What are the best lessons you learn from Judges? What does God say to you through this study? What do you think He says to your world?

Daily Life at Its Worst
And at Its Best

Before considering the message of Judges 17-21 and the book of
Ruth, let us be reminded of the fact that chapters 17-21 in Judges
are called an appendix or supplement to the Deuteronomic book of
Judges, which is basically 2:6—16:31 without the inclusion, perhaps,
of the minor judges. The introductory materials listed at the end of
this lesson will indicate the critical points of view. The material in
these chapters appears in its present form to supplement our understanding of the everyday life of the people of Israel during the period
of the judges. We accept the idea of the present book coming to us
after some modification, but in its final form a product of the guidance and direction of the Holy Spirit through the writers used to
complete the book.

Critical judgments about the book of Ruth vary all the way from
Robert H. Pfeiffer's proposal that this is a charming fictional ro-
mance, written about 400 B.C., which has no apparent purpose in
relation to Israel's history (*Introduction to the Old Testament,* pp.
717-718), to Edward J. Young's view that the book was composed
some time during the reign of David, having as one of its purposes
the tracing of the ancestry of David through a Moabitess (*Introduction to the Old Testament,* p. 358). Several scholars propose that
the purpose of this factual story or historical novel was to protest the
restrictions of Ezra-Nehemiah against mixed marriages after the
return of Israelites from the Babylonian Exile (for instance, G. W.

Thatcher, *Judges, Ruth,* The New Century Bible, pp. 176-178; George A. F. Knight in the Torch Bible Commentary, *Ruth and Jonah,* p. 21).

We believe that Ruth is a historical story, beautifully told, but passed down orally first, later in writing, and finally in the form in which it has come to us, probably from the time of the Jewish Exile. It has stood the test of time and has demonstrated through the centuries its ability to serve as an inspired writing through which God can speak to man. While we recognize the problems of interpretation, including the question of whether or not 4:18-22 was a part of the original, we believe that the book in its final form carries an understandable and unified message.

Instead of following the Hebrew Bible in placing Ruth among the later writings (which is where it probably belongs in terms of the date of composition), we have followed the Septuagint and English versions in studying Ruth in connection with the book of Judges. This is suggested in Ruth 1:1 and the book of Ruth manifestly belongs to this period in Israel's history even though it may have been committed to writing much later. Now let us turn our attention to the picture of daily life in that period.

DAILY BIBLE READINGS

MONDAY

Read Judges 17 and 18 prayerfully. Observe the story of Micah, his mother, the Levite, and the Danites against their primitive background. From Joshua 19:40-46 and Judges 1:34-36 we conclude that the Danites were unable to possess the territory south of Ephraim and near the Mediterranean coast. They were seeking living room, as were the Americans who moved westward from the eastern seaboard.

TUESDAY

Read chapter 19. Try to imagine the human situation behind this chapter. Note the geography involved, the delineation of character, the attitude toward women, and the beastly manner of some men. The contrast in the book of Ruth will stand out stronger because of this story.

WEDNESDAY

Read chapters 20 and 21 as a continuation of chapter 19. Observe where the men of Israel from the various tribes assembled, and the reaction of the Benjaminites. Most scholars believe that the number of fighting men is exaggerated. The plan and consequence of the fighting and the provision for wives may be noted.

THURSDAY

Read Ruth 1. Observe the striking contrast between the tone of Judges 17-21 and the book of Ruth. What makes verse 16 in its larger context a classic statement of loyalty? How did Naomi feel when she returned to Bethlehem? What does this chapter say to you?

FRIDAY

Read Ruth 2. Observe the steps by which Ruth gained the favor of Boaz. What elements of human interest do you find? Note the customs reflected through the book of Ruth.

SATURDAY

Read Ruth 3 and 4. Observe how Naomi the matchmaker and Boaz the lover move toward and accomplish the marriage of Boaz and Ruth. They acted in honor according to the customs of the time. Note the genealogy in Ruth 4:18-22, going back to Genesis 38:29 and 46:12.

SUNDAY

Review Judges and Ruth. Think through the book of Judges and then the book of Ruth for the message of these respective books. You may wish in this lesson to note some of the striking contrasts between Judges 17-21 and Ruth. Think, for instance, of Judges 19 and Ruth 3, or of the taking of Micah's priest and ephod, and Ruth's commitment to Naomi's God. Other contrasts will suggest themselves. Our headlines suggest similar contrasts today. Does not God still rule and over-rule to accomplish His purpose?

DETAILED STUDY

In our study of Judges 17-21, we propose to lift out the personal and tribal tragedy which came to Israel because there was no king in Israel, and every man did what was right in his own eyes. The point of view from which these chapters are written is either that of the kingdom of David actually, which would place this material during or soon after his reign, or the kingdom of David ideally, which might place the material during or after the Exile (587-538 B.C.), as many scholars propose.

A. THE TRAGEDY OF MICAH. Chs. 17; 18:17-26.

1. What was Micah's first sin? What led him to restore the stolen money to his mother? Observe what the mother did with the stolen money. This consecration of the money meant that it could be used for no other purpose. From the point of view of the covenant between God and His people, what was Micah's mother's mistake? What further sin did Micah commit concerning his image? Observe how he engaged in a tragedy of errors in his personal and religious life.

2. What was the Levite from Judah seeking? Observe the agreement made with him by Micah. Note also the fact that Micah felt good about his bargain, and that the Levite seems to be happy. Even though the shrine at which this priest served was in direct violation of the second commandment, Micah expected the Lord to prosper him. Note how his tragedy of errors builds up from one to the other.

3. We find the sequel to the story in 18:17-26. What did the spies of the Danites take from Micah when they returned to his house? Observe how the priest felt about serving the whole tribe rather than one man. When Micah learned of his loss, who went with him to help recover the stolen property? What were his words in verse 24? Why did he return home empty-handed? Note that Micah started by stealing and lost by theft. But his greater loss was his failure to understand the demands of the covenant, and his assumption that his gods could be stolen when he was presumably a worshiper of God. Yet how often our real gods, such as wealth or success, are taken from us, and we feel that we have lost everything. Can it be that Micah's tragedy is our own written in an ancient setting?

B. The Tragedy of the Levite and His Concubine.
Chs. 19; 20:1-7.

1. What family difficulty led the concubine of Bethlehem to return home from Ephraim? What was her husband's purpose when he went for her four months later? How long did he remain with his father-in-law? Note when they started back to Ephraim the city in which they stopped and the kindness shown them by an old man of Gibeah. This kind of hospitality is still shown by Jews and Arabs to strangers. Observe the host's proposal to protect his visitor, and the Levite's effort to save his own skin at the expense of his concubine. When did he discover that his concubine was dead? What did he do to arouse the men of Israel when he returned home? Where did they assemble to demand punishment of the men of Gibeah? The weakness of this Levite is shown in the repeated delay of his plans, the risk he was willing to take in starting late, and the sacrifice of his concubine to save his skin. Even though his society might have approved his actions, there was tragedy in his weakness. But every man did what was right in his own eyes, as Judges well says. This applies alike to the Levite and all others involved in the story.

C. The Tragedy of the Danites. Ch. 18.

1. As we have already observed, Joshua 19:40-47 and Judges 1:34-36 tell us that the Danites were unsuccessful in driving out the Canaanites from the area assigned to them. They were forced to look for living room elsewhere. Where did the spies of the Danites go? What was their report?

2. Note the reason for going to Laish and the new name given to the city. Who became their priests? (Some manuscripts have Gershom the son of Moses; others have Gershom the son of Manasseh.) Note the reference to Danites in 20:1.

D. The Tragedy of the Benjaminites. Chs. 20-21.

1. What request was made of the Benjaminites at Mizpeh? How did their response lead to civil war? Note the consequences of this war. Many scholars believe that the numbers of men in-

volved are exaggerated. What a price to pay for defending base men!

2. How is the concern of Israel for the tribe of Benjamin expressed at Bethel in 21:7? By what crude method did the Israelites propose to provide other daughters than their own for the Benjaminites to marry? By what other means did the Israelites provide wives for the Benjaminites? Benjamin was later identified with Judah, but Ezekiel 48 contains a reference to the portion of Benjamin as one of the twelve tribes of Israel. The tragedy of the Benjaminites is but a concrete illustration of the refrain of 21:25 in Judges.

E. LESSONS IN LIVING FROM JUDGES.

1. The consequences of incomplete obedience by the tribes of Israel, their series of oppressions and their inability to live in peace.

2. The grace and power of God in providing deliverers and in maintaining the Jewish people among enemies from without and from within during this strategic period in Israel's history.

3. The constant necessity for seeking solidarity as the people of God. Unity can be broken easily, as in the church today.

4. The personal and national or tribal tragedies which resulted from the fact that there was no unified leadership, such as a king in Israel. When every man does what is right in his own eyes, he usually does wrong.

5. The fact that the covenant people, however unaware of their obligations, still come under the requirement of obedience to God as their means of receiving His blessing.

F. SOCIAL CUSTOMS IN THE BOOK OF RUTH.

1. It is interesting to note the significance of the names in Ruth. Naomi probably means "my joy" or "my pleasantness"; Mara means "bitterness"; Ruth means "companion" or "friend"; and Boaz means "swiftness" or "strength."

2. To whom did Naomi suggest that Ruth and Orpah return in 1:8-13? Observe "her mother's house," as if to suggest the women's quarters; the possibility of a second marriage for

these daughters, and of sons under the Jewish law of Deuteronomy 25:5-6; the reference to Orpah's people and her gods in 1:15; and the striking contrast in 1:16-17.

3. Examine the events and customs concerning reaping in chapter 2. The reapers cut the grain, which was tied in bundles, probably by women, but some stalks were lost or left on the ground to be picked up by poor women or girls, especially the families of widows. Note Deuteronomy 24:19 in this connection, and the blessing which is promised.

4. Observe the special consideration shown by Boaz to Ruth. What special privileges is she to have by Boaz' command? Study the conversations between Ruth and Boaz. What do they reveal? How the tongues must have wagged at the invitation to lunch! Note how much barley Ruth took home with her.

5. Think through the conversation between Naomi the matchmaker and Ruth the willing young widow in 2:17-23. How little human nature has changed! Observe that Ruth stays where the gleaning is good and where prospects of a husband are equally good.

6. What is Naomi's plan when the time is ripe? What did she instruct Ruth to do? Note the time of day and the expected mood. Note the reference to the nearest of kin and the spreading of the skirt, which signifies protection. Observe the delicacy and charm with which Boaz recognizes another as the nearest of kin. (Had he done some investigation for just such a situation?) Six measures of barley have been variously estimated up to two bushels. Naomi saw in this pledge a promise of action.

7. Note the official action by ten witnesses to bless the marriage at the gate. Having discussed the matter privately with the nearest of kin, what did Boaz say to him publicly? What was his reply? By what sign did he release to Boaz his right of property and his right to marry Ruth? Observe the offspring of this happy marriage and the new happiness which came to Naomi. According to the genealogies in Matthew 1 and Luke 3, Boaz and Ruth also became the ancestor and ancestress of the

greater Son of Mary, the Word become flesh. The customs of ancient times were used by God to accomplish His eternal purpose.

G. THE PURPOSE OF GOD IN RUTH.

The book of Ruth serves as an excellent example of the way God's purpose was accomplished in troubled times. Ruth became the ancestress of David by God's plan.

1. What function did the famine of chapter 1 have in the story? The birth of sons and their marriage to Moabite women? The decision of Ruth to return with Naomi? The reference of Ruth to Naomi's people and Naomi's God in her reply in 1:16-17.

2. How did the events between Ruth and Boaz become a means of accomplishing the purpose of God? Note the character of Boaz as a factor also.

3. As you read chapter 2, observe the providence by which Ruth went to the field of Boaz. What is the greeting exchanged between Boaz and his workers in the field? Note how Ruth is identified in verse 6. Observe also how the special consideration given by Boaz and the special interest shown to Ruth is explained in verses 11-13. Observe Naomi's reply to the report from Ruth in verses 19-20. This forms the background for the remainder of the book.

4. Read chapters 3 and 4 as a unit, looking for steps by which the marriage of Ruth and Boaz and the birth of a son are consummated. What place has Levitate law in Naomi's plan? How does Boaz' kindness to Ruth prepare the way for the consummation of the marriage? In chapter 4, what legal steps are used to remove all obstacles to this marriage? How is the birth of a son recognized as a gift from God? The identification of Obed as the grandfather of David and the tracing of the ancestry back to Judah bring the statement of the purpose of God to a climax. The redemptive purpose of God is wrought out in the story of a family, one of whom is by marriage a converted foreigner or proselyte.

Thus the sordid stories of Judges find their counterpart in the beautiful and lovely story of Ruth. God was at work to redeem both man's failure and his faithfulness. This is the story of the Bible as a whole, being bound together by the outworking of the purpose of God as He works redemptively among His own people.

H. Lessons in Living from Ruth.

1. Suffering in the will of God may have a good purpose. Much depends on how suffering is received and the choices to which it leads us.
2. Loyalty to God is always honored in the long run. The results may not be evident immediately, but in the end they appear.
3. God's purpose is the key to the Old Testament and to history. This purpose works in individuals, in families, and in the nation.
4. The purpose of God may not be seen until after one or more generations. It may be seen in one's own experience. Keep on looking for it!

SUGGESTIONS FOR FURTHER READING

A. Commentaries:

Cooke, G. A., *The Book of Judges* (Cambridge Bible), pp. 156-197.
　　　　The Book of Ruth (Cambridge Bible).
The Interpreter's Bible, Vol. 2, pp. 798-852.
Knight, George A. F., *Ruth and Jonah* (Torch Bible Commentaries), pp. 1-45.
Moore, George F., *A Critical and Exegetical Commentary on Judges* (I.C.C.), pp. 365-454.
Rust, Eric C., *Judges, Ruth, I and II Samuel* (Layman's Bible Commentary, Vol. 6), pp. 59-76.
Thatcher, G. W., *Judges, Ruth* (The New Century Bible), pp. 141-195.

B. Introductory and Background Material:

Napier, B. Davie, *Song of the Vineyard,* pp. 145-146.
Pfeiffer, Robert H., *Introduction to the Old Testament,* pp. 717-719.
The Westminster Historical Atlas, revised edition, pp. 39-46.
Young, Edward J., *An Introduction to the Old Testament,* pp. 357-361.

QUESTIONS FOR THOUGHT AND DISCUSSION

1. What difference does our attitude toward Judges and Ruth as trustworthy accounts of God's message to man make in our learn-

ing from these books? In what sense does the message of the Bible transcend our ability to verify its historical accuracy in all details?

2. What do chapters 17-21 in Judges say about the need for a king in Israel? Do you think this is a clear indication that God approved this idea? Why or why not?

3. What can we learn about living from Judges 17-21? From the book of Judges as a whole? From the book of Ruth? How would you summarize the essential message of each of these books?

4. What can one family do to change the character of a nation? What difference did the family of Boaz and Ruth make on national life? Note the longer view of history here involved.

5. In what sense does God's plan become apparent as we look back over our own experience? Do we sometimes see how God's purpose is worked out after many days or years? What place do our choices have in our destiny? Think of Ruth's choice as an example.

6. Organize your own understanding of the relevance of these two books to the modern world. What makes them relevant? How may this relevance be shown?

Samuel, the Prophet of Israel

The book of Judges presents a picture of individualism and confusion in the life of Israel. It emphasizes the need for a central government and for an established code of morals for all Israel. The people moved from a military dictatorship under Joshua to what appears to have been a very loose tribal league. The order of the judges remains in force at the beginning of 1 Samuel, but Saul is anointed king by chapter 12. The latter part of the book emphasizes Saul's moral decline and the rise of David to power. In 2 Samuel David becomes the key figure, but in this part of 1 Samuel, the prophet Samuel is the key figure.

It may be noted that in the Hebrew Bible, both 1 and 2 Samuel were combined into one book, as were 1 and 2 Kings. The division into 1 and 2 Samuel (observe how the story of Saul's death is carried over into 2 Samuel 1) was made into the Septuagint translation, which was a Greek translation from the Hebrew between 250 and 150 B.C. Two scrolls were required for the Greek text, and since 1515 this division has appeared in the Hebrew Bibles. In the Greek and Latin Bibles, the four books of Samuel and Kings are described as I, II, III, and IV Kingdoms. Our translation follows Jerome's preference for 1 and 2 Samuel, 1 and 2 Kings.

AUTHORSHIP AND SOURCES

The authorship of the book of 1 Samuel, or at least part of it, cannot be attributed to Samuel. His death is recorded in 25:1 and the calling forth of his ghost is described in 28:8-19. Most scholars propose, without reference to a particular person, editors who used earlier and later sources, with a Deuteronomic edition at one stage of development. They do not generally follow Eissfelt in assigning three sources, P, J, and E, as a continuation of these sources in the first six books of the Old Testament, but rather propose earlier and later sources, a Deuteronomic edition, poetic fragments, such as the song of Hannah, and a miscellaneous appendix in chapters 21-24. A brief outline of proposed sources is given in the Layman's Bible Commentary, Vol. 6, pp. 78-79, and in *Harper's Bible Dictionary,* pp. 642-643. A conservative treatment is given in Edward J. Young's *An Introduction to the Old Testament,* pp. 188-189. More detailed treatments will be found in the sources proposed for further reading.

We would concur in Young's conclusion that "it seems obvious that the books were not completed in their present form until sometime after the division of the kingdom," that the author made use of previously existing documents, and that these are referred to in 1 Chronicles 29:29. We would agree further with his conclusion that the books of Samuel were composed "under divine inspiration by a prophet" but would allow for more than one prophet to have been used in the process.

Even though 1 Samuel appears to have raised many more problems than has 2 Samuel, primarily because of what are believed to be parallel accounts of the same incidents, we believe that the clue to understanding the writer or writers is not alone in the separation into different strands of material, but in a more careful apprehension of the personalities and characters involved. Most of us act "in character." Repetitions of events, for instance, while David was fleeing from Saul, do not necessarily prove that two sources were used. They may underline certain qualities of character in given types of situations. The final writer or writers may have used two accounts, but the purpose in so doing may well have been to present the character of the principal actors in the drama of redemption. From this point of view the separation or division into sources may distort rather than properly interpret the message that these books intended to convey. We must be careful to adapt ourselves to Hebrew modes of thought, not to force materials into our modern categories of thought as the basis of interpretation.

One further word may be said at this point. The setting forth of different points of view in the same book may be intentional. For instance, both Samuel's anointing of Saul in 1 Samuel 10 and his warning against demanding a king to be like other nations in chapters 8 and 12 may be the writer's way of saying that both points of view were understood to be God's will at this stage of Israel's history. This does not mean that a king is the best thing for Israel ideally, or that the reasons for wanting a king were right. Ideally, Israel was a theocracy, with no king but God. Practically, Israel needed a king who would serve as God's representative under the theocracy. If Saul failed in this capacity, David might succeed and set an example for his successors. Even though David proves weak upon occasion, God still controls history. We must interpret the Old Testament in terms of God's redemptive purpose, not in terms of our modern categories of analysis. The finished product is always more than the sum of the parts.

THE OVER-ALL STRUCTURE OF 1 SAMUEL

It will be helpful for each student to scan the book of 1 Samuel and to write down his own proposed chapter titles and divisions. He may then check his work in a good commentary. Here is one proposal:

A. SAMUEL, THE LAST JUDGE AND THE FIRST GREAT PROPHET OF ISRAEL (1:1—8:22).

   1. Samuel's birth and early childhood (1:1-23).
   2. Samuel's dedication to the service of the Temple under Eli (1:24—2:11).
   3. Eli's sons fail as judges over Israel (2:12-17).
   4. Samuel grows to boyhood (2:18-21, 26).
   5. Eli is warned concerning his sons' failure (2:22-25, 27-36).
   6. Samuel is called and continues to grow (ch. 3).
   7. The ark of God is captured by the Philistines, and later returned to Israel (4:1—7:2).
   8. Samuel calls for a renewal of the covenant at Mizpeh (7:3-17).

9. Samuel's sons fail as judges, and the people ask for a king (ch. 8).

B. SAMUEL FADES AS A POLITICAL LEADER AND SAUL BECOMES KING OF ISRAEL (9:1—12:25).

1. Samuel recognizes Saul as the future king of Israel (ch. 9).
2. Samuel anoints Saul privately as the new king (ch. 10).
3. Saul wins popular acclaim for his victory at Jabesh-gilead (ch. 11).
4. Samuel gives his farewell address as a political leader (ch. 12).

C. THE EARLY REIGN AND MORAL FAILURE OF SAUL (13:1—15:35).

1. Saul's battles with the Philistines and his moral failure to obey (13:1-15a).
2. Jonathan's courage and Saul's victory against the Philistine garrison at Michmash (13:15b—14:46).
3. Saul's victories over other enemies of Israel (14:47-52).
4. Saul's disobedience concerning the Amalekites and Samuel's prediction of his rejection by God (ch. 15).

D. SAUL FADES AND DAVID RISES IN POPULAR FAVOR (16:1—31:13).

1. Samuel anoints David as God's chosen king over Israel (16:1-13).
2. David becomes Saul's armor-bearer and minstrel (16:14-23).
3. David slays Goliath (ch. 17).
4. Saul becomes jealous of David (ch. 18).
5. Saul attempts to kill David, who flees from him (ch. 19).
6. David and Jonathan vow everlasting friendship (ch. 20).
7. David takes Goliath's sword from Nob as he flees from Saul (ch. 21).
8. Saul destroys the priests at Nob except for Abiathar, who escapes (ch. 22).
9. David, a fugitive in the wilderness, delivers Keilah from the Philistines (ch. 23).
10. David spares Saul's life at Engedi (ch. 24).
11. Samuel dies; David marries Abigail and Ahinoam (ch. 25).
12. David spares Saul's life at Ziph (ch. 26).

13. David flees to the Philistines (ch. 27).
14. Saul goes to the medium at Endor, and is warned of his coming defeat (ch. 28).
15. David is sent home from fighting against the Israelites (ch. 29).
16. David fights against the Amalekites and rescues his wives, dividing the spoils of victory (ch. 30).
17. Saul and his sons die in battle (ch. 31).

DAILY BIBLE READINGS

MONDAY

Read chapters 1-3. Examine these chapters from the point of view of human interest. The Nazirite vow, which is pertinent here, is described in Numbers 6:13-21.

TUESDAY

Read 4:1—7:2. Study the place of the ark of God in the story, and the striking contrast set up between the ark and Dagon the god of the Philistines. The tumors referred to were probably like those of the bubonic plague. Note the primitive means by which respect for the ark of God was achieved. The location of Kiriath-jearim is not certain, but it was probably within territory occupied by Israel.

WEDNESDAY

Read 7:3—8:22. What was the purpose of the assembly called at Mizpeh by Samuel? Observe the great fear of the Philistines, who were about to drive the Israelites out of Palestine. Note God's help and the celebration of victory over the Philistines. Observe also that Samuel's sons, like the sons of Eli, were not worthy of their calling. What was the outcome of the three-way conversation between God, Samuel, and the people of Israel?

THURSDAY

Read chapters 9-10. Observe the steps by which Saul was led to Samuel and anointed by him. Note the ecstatic experience which came to Saul, and his reply to his father's question a little later. How was Saul presented to the people as the Lord's anointed king? With what twofold reaction? Note that Samuel is still the strong man in Israel.

FRIDAY

Read chapters 11-12. How did Saul become a hero to Israel? Note how the kingdom was renewed at Gilgal, as it had been renewed at Mizpeh in chapter 7, and centered in Shiloh in chapters 1-4. Saul helped to unify the kingdom of Israel in its struggle for survival against the Philistines. Observe Samuel's farewell address, his view of God in history, his use of prayer, and his final instructions and warning.

SATURDAY

Read chapters 13 and 14. Observe how Israel is fighting against the Philistines and how the pressure is on Saul. Note the significance of Samuel's reproof of Saul. The place of 13:7b-15a and the text of 13:1 are treated in competent commentaries and should be consulted. Observe the great courage of Jonathan in the story of chapter 14. Consult commentaries on the meaning of the ark (or ephod) in 14:18. Observe how Jonathan was saved from death by his friends.

SUNDAY

Read chapter 15 carefully. Observe the command of God given to Israel, and Saul's incomplete obedience in his capture of the Amalekites. Observe how Samuel sought out Saul. What conversation ensued between these two leaders? What principle did Saul again enunciate? How did Saul indicate his repentance? With what effect? Note the bloody way in which Agag was killed. How is the final breach between Samuel and Saul indicated? Think through the first fifteen chapters of 1 Samuel. What things stand out in your mind as the major lessons in living taught in these chapters? Think through the major characters in the story and the way each stays in character. How would you evaluate Saul's character? Samuel as a leader of Israel?

DETAILED STUDY

We propose to lift out three major emphases in these chapters. These are: (1) The struggle for survival against the Philistines; (2) the guidance and the power of God; and (3) the theocracy and the monarchy, which is inextricably bound up with the relation between Samuel the prophet and Saul the king.

A. THE STRUGGLE FOR SURVIVAL AGAINST THE PHILISTINES.

The long-standing struggle between Israel and the Philistines, presented in dramatic fashion by the exploits of Samson, had a definite effect on Israel's desire for a king. The five kings of Gaza, Ashkelon, Ashdod, Ekron, and Gath were willing and able to work together in a common program of expansion. Unable to move toward Egypt, they moved eastward and northward into territory claimed by Israel, pushing the Danites out of their territory near the Mediterranean. The collapse of Egypt's empire at the death of Rameses III in 1144 B.C. released the Philistines from invasion by Egypt. The Israelites had no central government to resist the onslaughts and the penetrations of the Philistines. This probably was behind their desire for a king.

1. Examine chapter 4 carefully. Note the number of Israelites lost in the battle of Ebenezer. Note the place of the ark in the story, and the ideas expressed concerning the gods of Israel. Observe verse 9 and the suggestion it contains. How is the Philistine victory described in verses 10 and 11? John Bright calls this the decisive blow (about 1050 B.C.) which resulted— as archaeological evidence shows—in the capture of Shiloh, the placing of Philistine garrisons at strategic points in the land, and the deprivation of the Israelites from using metal weapons except under Philistine jurisdiction (*A History of Israel,* p. 165; note 1 Samuel 10:5; 13:3-4; 13:19-23). The death of Eli and his sons, the capture of the ark, and the naming of Phinehas' son Ichabod all testify to the devastating blow to the people of God. The story of the ark and Dagon, together with the return of the ark, is probably designed to show that, while Israel is defeated, God is still powerful and active.

2. Reread chapter 7 from this point of view. Note the conditional promise of verse 3. How did the gathering at Mizpeh provide an occasion for further hostilities from the Philistines? How did Samuel's sacrifice relate itself to the victory God gave His people? Observe that Israel is striving to free herself from Philistine bondage. See the commentaries for references to verses 14 and 15, which some believe were added later. The Philistines were still a threat to Israel.

3. Read 8:1-5 and 8:19-20. Observe how Samuel's sons failed, as Eli's sons had done, and that this points again to the desire for a king.
4. Read chapter 13 with the Philistine threat to Israel in mind. Note the number of persons who remained with Saul and Jonathan, before and after Jonathan defeated the garrison at Geba. Observe how the pressure mounts on Saul as his army is deserting, and leads to his sacrifice and subsequent reproof by Samuel.
5. Read chapter 14 with the struggle for survival against the Philistines in mind. Note Jonathan's victory at Michmash. Observe also the statement that some of the Israelites were on the side of the Philistines and some were in hiding in verses 21-23. Observe also the summary of Saul's battles in 14:37-48.

These passages show clearly that the struggle for survival led to the demand for a monarchy, and that Samuel was the major proponent of the ideals of the theocracy in Israel.

B. THE THEOCRACY AND THE MONARCHY.

Let us first define what we mean by these terms. By theocracy we mean the government by God over a people or a nation. This may be extended to include priests or prophets as spokesmen for God, but this is not the essential or primary meaning, for priests and prophets may fail to understand or to declare the whole will of God. By monarchy we mean the government of a nation or a people by a monarch or king. The latter ordinarily includes a capitol and an established court (usually also a police force and an army) from which the nation is ruled.

We may also recognize the fact that most critical scholars propose two or three narratives embedded in the material to be examined. John Bright separates these clearly as 1 Samuel 9:1—10:16, continued in 13:3b, 4b-15. Woven in with this is the original separate account of chapter 11. The other strand comprises chapters 8; 10:17-27; 12. (See his *A History of Israel,* pp. 166-167, and compare commentaries listed for a similar assignment of materials.) Concerning the second strand we would agree with Bright in his statement: "But it is unsound to dismiss the last of these narratives as a reflection of subsequent bitter experience with the monarchy, as so many have done." Bernhard Anderson's *Understanding the Old Testament,* p. 119, should also be read in this connection. We are convinced that the inclusion of both points of view was intended by the author or authors, and that the monarchy was received with mixed feelings from the start. Let us see how these points of view are presented.

1. Read chapter 8 carefully. Recall its present position following the deliverance described in chapter 7. Note the basic request of verses 4-5. What hopes have been eliminated in the minds of the elders? What was God's answer to Samuel's prayer? Who had been rejected? How has this rejection been chronic? What was Samuel to do, not as the ideal solution to the problem, but as the best thing under the circumstances? What dangers inhered in having a king? According to verses 19-20, what was the reply of the people to Samuel's warning? When Samuel repeated these words to God, what was the second answer? Did Samuel appoint a king forthwith? What did he do? This will set up the narrative of 9:1—10:16, which precedes the public choosing of Saul by lot as king, as reported in 10:17-27.

Observe the situation here described. Israel is under terrific pressure from the Philistines, and there is no hope for the nation from judges or priests, and Samuel the prophet can give no military leadership. The elders see a choice between slavery and a king to lead them. Samuel the prophet, deliberating in prayer to God, sees the necessity of leadership but also the dangers inherent in an earthly king. Anyone as well informed as he was could have given the warning reported in 8:10-18 (just as we do not have to wait for fifty years to tell what Communist Russia will do to a nation). Samuel feared the perversion of the theocracy to a self-sustained monarchy. History bore him out. The further study of 2 Samuel and of 1 and 2 Kings will indicate how the promises concerning the seed of David almost displaced the covenant promises to God's people. What was wrong with the request? The reason was wrong. The people wanted to be like other nations when they were called to be different from other nations. They wanted a *man* they could trust in the place of God. Not by God's choice, but by His permission, they got what they wanted.

2. We have already examined chapter 9 in detail under the theme of God's guidance. Let us look at 10:1-16 more carefully. What was said to Saul concerning his mission at this private anointing? What special signs were given to indicate that this was God's anointing and not just Samuel's? Note 10:9 especially. The special gift of prophesying was considered a mark of God's presence among the prophets. This school of prophets, similar in some respects to those of other nations, had some kind of ecstatic experience in connection with worship. Except for the occasion in 19:18-24, Samuel did not associate with them as a group as far as we know, but he did recognize that their gift was from God.

3. The next stage in the story is that of a public anointing and setting up of the requirements of the kingdom. Read 10:17-27 carefully. In what context did Samuel call the people to present themselves as tribes at Mizpeh? Note the reminder that they have continually rejected God. How was Saul chosen to be king? Where was he found? What was his appearance when brought before the people? One might well think of Samson in this connection. How did Samuel present Saul, according to verse 24? How did the people react? Observe what Samuel did after this. Who indicated an unwillingness to follow Saul as king? Observe that there was no machinery of government, and that there was no capital city to which Saul might go. Saul would have to prove himself worthy of leadership in a manner similar to that of the judges who preceded him.

4. Read chapter 11 with this necessity in mind. What occasion enabled Saul to prove himself worthy of leadership? What did Nahash propose as a means of disgrace to Israel? Observe how Saul heard of their plight and summoned an army from Israel. Observe also Saul's message to the men of Jabesh-gilead. By what strategy did Saul defeat the Ammonites? With what result? How did Saul show good judgment in not punishing

those who had previously refused to follow him as king? Many scholars believe that verses 14 and 15 were added later to provide a transition from this account to that of chapter 12.

5. Read chapter 12 from the point of view of the theocracy and the monarchy. Examine Samuel's review of Israel's history. Note the reference to the deliverance from Egypt and from the enemies in Canaan under the judges. Why is verse 10 appropriate? Observe the reference to the monarchy and the theocracy in verse 12. Under what conditions would the king and the kingdom be blessed by God? How is this repeated and underlined in verses 19-25?

The requirements are here clearly set forth for the kingdom under the theocracy. If both king and people obey God, all will be well. If king or people disobey, punishment is sure to follow. Thus the covenant relationship which exists between God and His people is not taken away under the monarchy. Will the king obey? This is the focal question to be answered.

6. Read chapter 13 for understanding the context of verses 8-15. Observe the extreme pressure on Saul. Note Samuel's reproof of Saul for putting his judgment above God's command. Saul would use God to hold the people and to gain a victory. Samuel would have Saul used by God. This is a very important difference, not only for Saul but for us.

7. Read chapter 15 carefully. This is a key chapter in 1 Samuel. When Saul went against Agag under special orders, he was not concerned about survival, but something else. We may question the *hērem* (devotion to destruction) in the name of God. This was a primitive society in which God's will was so understood. Accepting this as God's will, what did Saul do about it? Study again the conversation between Samuel and Saul in verses 10-23 and the principle stated by Samuel in verses 22-23. After Saul had made a petition, what were Samuel's final words in verses 26-29? Note Saul's final request in verse 30, Samuel's killing of Agag, and the final judgment of Samuel and of God in verses 34-35.

The difficulty with the monarchy under Saul was that it became a substitute for the theocracy. Some scholars feel that

Samuel's personal feelings rather than God's judgment are primary here. We recognize Samuel's feelings, but believe that God's judgment is primary. Saul has demonstrated that he is not a man after God's own heart and that in God's sight he has not lived up to his highest opportunity. "To obey is better than sacrifice, and to hearken than the fat of rams." This is the final word concerning the theocracy and the kingdom in this part of 1 Samuel. The kingdom waits for a man willing to obey as king.

D. LESSONS IN LIVING.

1. The danger of personal failure in public life. Many public servants feel that their private life has nothing to do with their public service. Nothing could be further from the truth. Eli's sons and Samuel's sons serve as examples.

2. The relation of foresight to public policy. Samuel had such foresight. The elders lacked it.

3. The tendency to trust man rather than God. This is always a threat to any people, particularly in a time of fear.

4. The danger of trying to use God to accomplish personal or national goals. Saul reached the point where he believed that what was good for the nation must be good for God. Let us beware of similar thinking.

5. The fact that every nation is always under judgment by God. We are no exception.

6. The importance of obedience to God at all times. We may misread His will, but we dare not disobey it.

SUGGESTIONS FOR FURTHER READING

A. COMMENTARIES:

The Interpreter's Bible, Vol. 2, pp. 854-965.

Kennedy, A. R. S., ed., *The Books of Samuel* (The New Century Bible), pp. 3-116.

Kirkpatrick, A. F., *The First Book of Samuel* (Cambridge Bible), pp. 9-148.

Rust, Eric C., *Judges, Ruth, I and II Samuel* (Layman's Bible Commentary, Vol. 6), pp. 77-106.

Smith, H. P., *A Critical and Exegetical Commentary on the Books of Samuel* (I.C.C.), Introduction and pp. 3-143.

B. INTRODUCTORY AND BACKGROUND MATERIAL:

Anderson, Bernhard W., *Understanding the Old Testament,* pp. 114-121.
Bright, John, *A History of Israel,* pp. 163-171.
            The Kingdom of God, pp. 32-35.
Napier, B. Davie, *From Faith to Faith,* pp. 108-130.
            Song of the Vineyard, pp. 147-152.
Pfeiffer, Robert H., *Introduction to the Old Testament,* pp. 338-347.
The Westminster Historical Atlas, revised edition, pp. 47-51.
Wright, G. Ernest, *Biblical Archaeology,* pp. 120-123; abridged edition, pp. 66-69.
Young, Edward J., *An Introduction to the Old Testament,* pp. 188-199.

QUESTIONS FOR THOUGHT AND DISCUSSION

1. When should one pray for something he very much wants, as Hannah wanted a son? In what spirit should such a prayer be made?

2. Why is it hard for children of a good father to carry on the family tradition? How may parents help children to find their vocation and service?

3. How does one's culture affect one's religious outlook? One's faith? One's view of God and the world? One's sense of destiny? Illustrate from 1 Samuel.

4. What is your view concerning the critical problems in 1 Samuel? Does the search for accurate knowledge increase or decrease your reverence for God and your confidence in the Bible? Why?

5. In what sense could God approve Saul as king and yet disapprove Saul's later conduct? What is meant by God's repenting of His previous actions?

6. What are the three most significant things these chapters say to you? Why these? How can you make them meaningful to someone else? Try it!

The Conflict Between David and Saul

In these chapters the fading splendor of Saul is matched by the rising star of David. It appears that two distinct strands are interwoven in the text, with possible additions, to give the message intended by the inspired writer. As a typical effort to assign sources, we may take the proposal of H. P. Smith, *The Books of Samuel* (I.C.C.), Introduction, pp. xxii-xxvi:

1. To one source, probably the Samuel source: 16:1-13; 17:1—18:5; 18:14-19; 18:30—19:10; 19:18-24; 21:11-16; 22:3-5; 23:11—24:26; 28; 31.
2. To the other source, probably the Saul source: 16:14-23; 18:6-13, 20-29a; 19:11-17; 21:2-10; 22:1-2, 6-23; 23:1-14; 25; 26; 27; 29; 30; 2 Samuel 1.
3. As a fragment from another source: ch. 20 and perhaps 21:1.

This is only one of several attempts to harmonize duplicate accounts of similar events. We must recognize the strong probability that different sources have been used, and that this may account for the apparent confusion or discrepancies in the text. However, we would go one step beyond such analysis to inquire what message is imparted in the final composition that we know as 1 Samuel 16—2 Samuel 1. This is our primary question. The book says something in its present form. To that message we now would address ourselves, being reminded of the over-all structure proposed on page 60 above.

DAILY BIBLE READINGS

Monday

Read chapters 16-18 prayerfully. Observe how these chapters follow the account of Saul's reign in chapters 8-15. It may be less confusing to read 16:1-13; 17:1—18:5, and then to read 16:14-23 just prior to 18:6—19:24. Following this order, observe the requirements met by David as the future king of Israel. Note also that the Spirit of God came upon him mightily from that day forward. As you read 17:1—18:5, observe the steps by which David became a national hero. According to 16:14-23, how did David become a member of Saul's guard? Why did Saul become jealous of David, as indicated in 18:6-9? How did Saul express his jealousy? Note the two cases where he sought to have David killed by fighting against the Philistines.

Tuesday

Read chapters 19 and 20. How did Jonathan's friendship help to protect David from Saul? Compare 18:1-5. Observe Saul's promise to Jonathan and his later period of melancholy. How did Michal save David? Where did David flee? What does the story of Samuel and the prophets at Naioth say to you? Observe that Samuel is here associated with a company of prophets. How did Jonathan warn David in chapter 20? Note Saul's strong disapproval of Jonathan's friendship with David. What does this friendship between Jonathan and David teach us?

Wednesday

Read chapters 21-23. What kind of bread did David receive at Nob? What else did he receive there? Note the reference to Doeg the Edomite in verse 7. Observe how David escaped Achish the king of Gath and assembled four hundred fighting men. Observe also how Saul killed the men of Nob except for Abiathar who escaped, and the place Doeg had in the story. What promise did David make to Abiathar? Why did David rescue Keilah from the Philistines? How did he escape Saul once more? Note the renewal of the covenant between Jonathan and David in 23:15-18. Observe also that David escaped Saul again when he was betrayed by the Ziphites. Where did David then go?

THURSDAY

Read chapters 24-26. Why did David refuse to kill Saul in the cave at Engedi? Locate these places on a map. What did David say to Saul later? Observe Saul's reply. Do you think he meant what he said? Did his jealousy overtake him later? Observe how David secured Abigail as his wife, and that he married another woman as well. What was done with Michal? We cannot condone the practice of having more than one wife in the light of Jesus' teaching. It was the accepted practice in David's time. As you read chapter 26, note who betrayed David's hiding place to Saul. Under what circumstances did David spare Saul's life a second time? What did David say to Abner and to Saul? What was Saul's reply? With what immediate result? Many scholars take chapters 24 and 26 as two accounts of the same incident. We have interpreted them as two incidents.

FRIDAY

Read chapters 27-29. Why did David finally go to the king of Gath? Observe his request. How did David and his men survive during this period? What position was offered to David by the king of Gath? Under what circumstances? Observe Saul's special effort to secure a message from God, and the lengths to which he went. What message did he receive from the ghost of Samuel through the witch of Endor? Note the effect of this message on Saul. What did the woman do to revive Saul's spirits? According to chapter 29, how was David saved from fighting against Israel?

SATURDAY

Read chapters 30 and 31. Observe what David found when he returned to Ziklag. What instructions did he receive? Note the information received from an abandoned Egyptian. How did David recover the spoils of war? What principle did he establish in dividing with those who were left behind? Note the account of the death of Saul's sons and of Saul himself. What did the Philistines do with Saul's head and armor? What did the men of Jabesh-gilead then do?

SUNDAY

Read 2 Samuel 1. Observe how Saul's death was reported to David and by whom. Compare this report with that given in 1 Samuel 31.

Why did David have the Amalekite slain? Examine the lamentation of David carefully.

DETAILED STUDY

Several fruitful topics suggest themselves for further study. We propose to consider the decline of Saul, the rise of David, and the friendship between David and Jonathan. In these and other topics we will become increasingly aware of the way God's purpose is worked out in Israel.

A. THE DECLINE OF SAUL.

In some senses Saul is one of the most tragic characters of the Old Testament. He was not born to greatness. He never became fully adequate for the large responsibilities of the king of Israel. It may be argued that Samuel prevented him from achieving the greatness of which he was capable. There can be little doubt that the break between Samuel and Saul described in 1 Samuel 15 had a bad psychological effect on Saul. With the great odds he faced, such as the danger from the Philistines, the lack of unity among the tribes of Israel, the absence of any traditions of kingship, and the possible expectation of the people that he should keep his charismatic gifts, Saul faced an almost impossible task. He might have achieved a larger measure of temporary success with the continued support of Samuel and with the wholehearted support of all Israel. His mental disturbances might have been less frequent or less severe under less pressure.

The account in 1 Samuel, however, is geared to deeper levels of thought. The monarchy was established under the theocracy, and any movement toward independence from God meant ultimate disaster for the nation. To violate the prerogatives of the priesthood, as in chapter 13, or to violate the *hērem* (things devoted to God), as in chapter 15, may not appear to be so wrong in themselves. But they point direction just as does a weather vane. Under pressure Saul will be like kings of other nations and not like a king under God. This tendency, together with his frustration in feeling that he had lost the Spirit of God, serves as the clue to the failure of Saul. Let us see how this movement toward failure is presented in 1 Samuel 16-31.

1. Read 1 Samuel 16:14-16 carefully. Note the twofold statement in verse 14. What effect did the evil spirits have on Saul? What cure did his servants propose?

Let us make a few observations about Saul's sickness. *First,* it followed after Saul's second major sin as the leader of God's people. In 15:24-31 Saul repents and returns to God, apparently recognizing the basic principle stated in 15:22-23. Saul was quick to repent, which was commendable. But he was not able to carry through and remain true to his repentance. His melancholy followed his consciousness that he had gone contrary to God's will. *Second,* the departure of the Spirit of God cannot be assumed to be an arbitrary withdrawal from a man who strives to live in His conscious presence, but rather the consequence of a man who decides to go his own way. We know this experience too well to argue the point. *Third,* it is also true to human experience that when we forsake God as Lord, an evil spirit or many evil spirits, as it were, take hold of us. We never live in a spiritual vacuum. Jesus illustrates this truth in the parable recorded in Luke 11:24-26, where the unclean spirit was cast out but returned with seven others worse than himself. *Fourth,* in describing Saul's experience as the Spirit of God leaving him and as evil spirits coming upon him (at first sporadically), the Jewish mind is speaking. This mind attributed everything that happened to God. It dealt with the ultimate Cause and frequently made no mention of secondary causes. We westerners would use psychological terms like "depression" or "insecurity." But this need not keep us from understanding the deep spiritual experience described by Hebrew writers. A *fifth* word may also be said. While it is true that a doctrine of demons had not been developed in Jewish theology up to this point, this does not prevent any writer from using terms that describe certain types of experience. For instance, writers used the term "depression" long before it became a key word in modern psychology and psychiatry. While therefore we cannot communicate in words the exact nature of Saul's emotional and mental disturbance, we may at least approach an understanding of it. The spiritual experience which lacked proper moorings led to mental and emotional disorders which lacked proper direction or coherence. Saul needed a transforming and enabling experience with God. He needed more than self-analysis of his melancholy or music to drive it away.

2. Read 1 Samuel 17:8-11. What effect did the taunts of Goliath have on Saul and the people of Israel? What does a dynamic faith do to bolster courage? What does its absence do to take away courage?

3. Note the occasion of Saul's jealousy in 18:6-9. To what fear did this jealousy lead him? Read the remainder of chapters 18-20, noting the various devices used by Saul to accomplish David's death. For instance: 18:10-11; 18:17-19; 18:20-29; 19:1; 19:8-10; 19:11-17; 19:18-24; 20:30-34. Observe the intensity of Saul's jealousy and the deterioration of his character with his one obsession to get rid of David by one means or another, preferably in a way that would not hurt Saul politically. New let us examine some of the efforts of Saul to take David's life in the chapters that follow.

4. What means did Saul use to punish Ahimelech the priest in 22:1-19? Who escaped and reported to David in 22:20-23?

5. What use did Saul propose to make of the Ziphites in 23:19-24? Observe how David was again delivered from Saul.

6. Read chapter 24 again. Why did David spare Saul? What reply did Saul make, according to 24:16-22? Observe what Saul did afterwards. He had good impulses, but found it hard to stay with them.

7. Read the similar passage in chapter 26 again. Observe both the similarity and the difference in details. You may wish to get these on paper. Observe that David refused again to kill the king of Israel, and Saul's response in 26:21-25.

8. With dramatic insight, the inspired writer presents the spiritual death of Saul in chapter 28 before presenting his physical death in chapter 31. The two are closely related, as chapter 28 indi-

cates. According to 28:3-7, what effect did the Philistine armies have on Saul? By what means did he fail to make contact with God? In what contradictory position did he find himself in seeking aid from a medium? What message did the spirit of Samuel give Saul in verses 15-19? How does the beginning of Saul's downfall come again into the picture? Note the emphasis on Saul's disobedience. According to verses 20-25, what effect did this message from Samuel have on Saul? With faith gone, and fellowship with God gone, Saul had little left to give him courage.

9. How is Saul's tragic death described in chapter 31? Who died with him? How did the Philistines insult him in death? What did the men of Jabesh-gilead do to show him honor?

Saul's loss of nerve came from within. Granting the outward pressures upon him, we must recognize also that his jealousy and his moods of despondency combined to make Saul the king behave like a frightened youth or a spoiled child. His fear grew out of his loss of faith. Possessed by the qualities of physical vigor and quickness to recognize his own weakness, Saul lacked withal the strong purpose and self-discipline required to serve as a king under God. This was the task to which he was called, and the task in which he failed. We now turn to a man whose rise to power parallels Saul's decline.

B. DAVID'S RISE TO POWER.

1. Read 16:1-13 again from the point of view of the beginning of David's rise to power. Note especially verses 7 and 12. What qualities did David possess? What is added in verse 13? Observe the contrast suggested in verse 14 and the favor found by David in verses 14-23.

2. We have already recognized the possible use of at least two sources in the story of David and Saul in chapters 16-31. Now read chapter 17. With this dramatic event David became a hero among the people. This is nowhere more clearly expressed than in 18:5, where both Saul and the people recognize David's ability, and in 18:6-7, which gave rise to Saul's intense jealousy. Observe these chapters again, and the way David was delivered

from a series of efforts by Saul to have him killed, or to deliver the fatal blow himself. Note the explanation for David's continued success in 18:12, 14-15, 28, 30.

3. In chapter 21, David was given food by Ahimelech (which cost Ahimelech dearly) and feigned madness before Achish the king of Gath. What question was asked in verse 11 to indicate David's prestige even among the Philistines? Observe also in chapter 22 the motley group who surrounded David.

4. In chapter 23, while David was living like a fugitive in "no man's land," in what specific ways did he receive instruction from the Lord? With what results? Note this element in his experience, which is in striking contrast with Saul's experience recorded in chapter 28.

5. In chapters 24 and 26, examine these stories again for the reasons why David spared Saul's life in each case. Note his respect for the office of the king, and the questions and comments which help interpret this feeling even while Saul seeks David's life. This would seem to be excellent public relations with the people of Israel. The story of chapter 25, especially verses 23-35, suggests the guidance of God also.

6. Chapter 27 reports an unflattering chapter in David's career as an outlaw. To the Jewish mind, what would indicate the hand of God in these raids? Note verses 4 and 12. This is also preparation for 28:1-2. What did Achish do for David?

7. According to chapter 29, how did David escape the necessity for fighting against his own people? Observe how God's hand is in this decision. It will be doubly important in later times.

8. Read chapter 30 from the point of view of David's rise to power. Note his seeking of God's guidance, his kindness to the Egyptian, his recovery of the spoils, and his wisdom in sharing them with the men who remained in the camp. Note also verses 26 and 31. Observe on a map the general location of these places mentioned, and note the fact that Hebron is among them. Hebron was David's first capital.

9. Read 2 Samuel 1:1-16 for its picture of David's respect for Saul as king. Note the cruel treatment of the Amalekite and the reason given for it. Read verses 17-27 for David's lament over

Saul and Jonathan. What good things did he say about both? How, indeed, were the mighty fallen in battle! And how great the loss to Israel as well as to David in the death of Jonathan! David's sorrow was genuine, but he did not lose any votes in his public expression of it.

The rise of David in this part of the Old Testament therefore reaches its climax in the death of Saul the king and of Jonathan the heir apparent. David, of course, has previously been anointed as the future king, but Samuel the prophet is not alive to testify to this act. It remains for David's friends to take the initiative after the death of Saul. Thus far David has received the protection and the blessing of God under circumstances much more trying than those faced by Saul. Adversity broke Saul's spirit, but strengthened the spirit of David. In his adversity David had a rich friendship with Saul's son Jonathan, and to that friendship we now turn our attention.

C. The Friendship of David and Jonathan.

1. Read 19:1-7. What special favor did Jonathan show David some time after Saul's jealousy had been kindled?
2. Chapter 20 is devoted wholly to this friendship. Read it carefully, noting in verses 1-11 a situation similar to that described in 19:1-7. What plan is devised between David and Jonathan? Verses 12-17 are at the heart of this chapter. What covenant did David and Jonathan make? How is their mutual love described? Observe the plan made in verses 18-23. What was Saul's reaction to David's absence at the feast, as reported in verses 24-29? Verses 30-34 tell us the price Jonathan was willing to pay for his friendship with David. Observe his willingness to give up his succession to the throne, his temporary break with his father, and his temporary danger from his father because of Saul's jealousy over David. This friendship went deep in Jonathan's heart. Note how it is sealed once again in verses 35-42, and the reference to the descendants of these two friends.
3. Read 23:14-18. Note that Jonathan came to David while he was a fugitive from Saul, and that Saul had to find someone besides Jonathan to betray David's whereabouts. Jonathan went home,

refusing to go after David with his father. Observe what Jonathan says to David in verse 17.

4. Study 2 Samuel 1 for what is said about Jonathan in David's lamentation. Observe how verse 26 sums up a deep sense of loss for a friend whose love was lasting and deep.

It is apparent that, in spite of the great tension between Saul and David, the king's son and the anointed future king were devoted friends until Jonathan's untimely death. The jealousy which marked Saul's fading splendor did not spread to the heart of Jonathan. Jonathan was a worthy son of a sick father. He has written his courage and unselfishness clearly on the pages of Hebrew history. The rise of David in no sense eclipses the devotion and courage of his friend Jonathan, one of the mighty who fell defending the Israel he loved.

It is proper here to recognize that the covenant between God and His people is not a major element in the story. After all, the story of these chapters is the story of Saul and David. It is not primarily that of the people of the covenant.

D. LESSONS IN LIVING.

1. Keep your devotional life in good order. This is not merely a matter of engaging in prayers or worship, but also of obedience to the will of God. Disobedience breaks contact with God quickly, as Saul's experience testifies.

2. Cultivate redemptive and lasting friendships. The friendship between David and Jonathan was good for them and serves as a challenging example for us.

3. Wait in God's will for His plan to be worked out. David, the Lord's anointed, did not rush matters, even though he might have been justified in claiming self-defense when killing Saul. His respect for the office of king gave David respect and helped him keep his self-respect.

4. Work out your own further lessons in living. Let 1 Samuel become a means by which God speaks to you for daily living.

SUGGESTIONS FOR FURTHER READING

A. COMMENTARIES:

The Interpreter's Bible, Vol. 2, pp. 965-1048.

Kennedy, A. R. S., ed., *The Books of Samuel* (The New Century Bible), pp. 116-197.

Kirkpatrick, A. F., *The First Book of Samuel* (Cambridge Bible), pp. 147-246.

Rust, Eric C., *Judges, Ruth, I and II Samuel* (Layman's Bible Commentary, Vol. 6), pp. 106-123.

Smith, H. P., *A Critical and Exegetical Commentary on the Books of Samuel* (I.C.C.), pp. 143-265.

B. INTRODUCTORY AND BACKGROUND MATERIAL:

Anderson, Bernhard W., *Understanding the Old Testament*, pp. 122-135.
Bright, John, *A History of Israel*, pp. 171-174.
Napier, B. Davie, *Song of the Vineyard*, pp. 152-153.
Pfeiffer, Robert H., *Introduction to the Old Testament*, pp. 347-351.
Wright, G. Ernest, *Biblical Archaeology*, pp. 123-129; abridged edition, pp. 69-75.

QUESTIONS FOR THOUGHT AND DISCUSSION

1. What should a person do when he fears he is "losing his grip" and feels forsaken by God?
2. What causes jealousy? What is the best cure for it? What does it do to human personality unless it is overcome? What did it do to Saul?
3. How should one take unfair treatment from superiors? From equals? How did David's treatment by Saul help to prepare him for his later experiences as king of Israel?
4. Why is it hard to wait for God's purpose to be worked out in our lives? What does 1 Samuel teach us about patience in the will of God?
5. What are some of the values of friendship? How do we develop lasting friendships? Illustrate from 1 Samuel.
6. How could David be a man after God's own heart and still do some of the things he did, such as marrying more than one wife, demanding a gift from Nabal, killing Amalekites and the Amalekite who brought news of Saul's death? In what sense does the Old Testament reflect its own world view? How should we interpret it in the light of the Christian gospel?
7. What are the most significant things you learn from 1 Samuel?

David's Expansion
of Israel

Second Samuel tells the story of David's expansion and consolidation of Israel and of the difficulties he faced in holding the state together. These difficulties were related to his sin against Uriah and the succession to his throne. We do well to keep in mind the fact that this is an interpretation of history showing how God works in Israel's history.

Even though they differ on details, most scholars assign the major portion of chapters 9-20 to Abiathar or some other scribe who wrote the memoirs of David's court soon after the accession of Solomon. Much of chapters 2-8 is assigned to the Saul source, with chapter 6 to a combination of Samuel and Saul sources, and with considerable controversy over chapter 7. Chapters 21:1-4 and 24 may be from the same source as chapters 9-20, but on this scholars are not agreed. Some ascribe the poems in chapters 22 and 23 to David. Eric C. Rust agrees with this but regards chapters 21-24 as a miscellaneous appendix added to the books of Samuel (Layman's Bible Commentary, Vol. 6, p. 79). H. P. Smith and *The Interpreter's Bible* give a somewhat detailed treatment of critical problems. Edward J. Young differs with most of the views expressed above and affirms the essential unity of 2 Samuel (*Introduction to the Old Testament*, pp. 197-199). Young's explanation of the slaying of Goliath in 1 Samuel 17:49 and of the apparently conflicting statement in 2 Samuel 21:19 comes from 1 Chronicles 20:5, where Elhanan is credited with slaying the brother of Goliath.

From the evidence cited we may conclude that the major portion of 2 Samuel (with chapters 9-20 as a minimum) comes from the hand of an inspired writer who lived close to or during the time of the events interpreted, with other parts included to complete the story. We study the text with confidence that God is speaking through it.

THE OVER-ALL STRUCTURE OF 2 SAMUEL

It is always helpful for the student to work out his own outline of each book of the Bible. The exercise of determining structure and giving titles to chapters helps students to think through the material. Here is one possible outline.

I. THE REIGN OF DAVID OVER JUDAH (chs. 1-4).

    A. David's lament over Saul and Jonathan (ch. 1).
    B. Rival kingdoms, David versus Ishbosheth (chs. 2:1—3:5).
    C. Steps leading to Ishbosheth's death in Israel (chs. 3:6—4:12).

II. THE REIGN OF DAVID OVER ALL ISRAEL (chs. 5-24).

    A. David's rise to power over Israel (chs. 5-10).
        1. Tribes make David king over all Israel; he captures Jerusalem (ch. 5).
        2. David brings the ark to Jerusalem (ch. 6).
        3. God's promise to make David a house (ch. 7).
        4. David extends his kingdom (ch. 8).
        5. David shows kindness to Mephibosheth (ch. 9).
        6. David extends his kingdom to Syria (ch. 10).
    B. David's sin and near loss of his kingdom (chs. 11-18).
        1. David's sin against Uriah (ch. 11).
        2. Nathan's reproof—trouble will come out of David's own house (ch. 12).
        3. Absalom avenges abuse of Tamar (ch. 13).
        4. Joab secures Absalom's recall to Jerusalem (ch. 14).
        5. Absalom rebels against David, who flees Jerusalem (ch. 15).
        6. Absalom claims the palace as king (ch. 16).
        7. David's army in array against Absalom's army (ch. 17).
        8. Joab defeats and kills Absalom (ch. 18).
    C. David's return to his kingdom (chs. 19-20).

    1. David received in Jerusalem as king of all Israel (ch. 19).

    2. Joab kills Amasa; crushes Sheba's rebellion (ch. 20).

  D. Miscellaneous facts about David's kingdom (chs. 21-24).

    1. The sons of Saul; Rizpah's devotion (ch. 21).

    2. David's song of deliverance (ch. 22).

    3. David's swan song; his mighty men (ch. 23).

    4. David numbers Israel and Judah (ch. 24).

Certain larger movements may be observed. *First,* David as king over Judah has a rival king in Israel. Through a series of providential acts he becomes king of all Israel. With the help of the loyal Joab, he extends his kingdom over all of Palestine and even beyond its borders. Then through personal sin he almost loses his kingdom to Absalom, but he is sustained and returns to rule again over all Israel. This is not without opposition, however. The miscellaneous material in chapters 21-24, although undated, appears to belong to certain times during the reign of David described in the earlier part of the book. Now let us turn our attention to chapters 1-12, with chapters 13-24 to be examined in the next lesson.

DAILY BIBLE READINGS

The care with which each student does the daily Bible readings will determine the value of this study for him. The additional study and suggested readings are designed to supplement these readings, but not to serve as a substitute for them.

MONDAY

Read chapter 1 again. In what ways does this chapter prepare the way for David to become king of Judah and of all Israel? Note how it introduces the movement of the book as a whole.

TUESDAY

Read chapters 2-4. Observe the location of the two rival kingdoms. The Philistines probably controlled most of the western part of Palestine, and may have preferred a divided Israel. Note also how the jousting party led to open hostility and how the jealousy of Abner led to the establishment of David as king over all Israel. David's political astuteness may also be observed.

WEDNESDAY

Read chapters 5 and 6. Observe the reference to groups coming to crown David in 5:1, 2, and 3. Note also the length of David's reign. First Chronicles 11:1-9 may be read in this connection, for it also gives an account of the capture of Jerusalem, which came permanently under control of Israel at this time. What did the Philistines do when they saw David consolidating his kingdom? Observe how David sought guidance from God, who gave victory over the Philistines. The unhappy experience with Michal when David brought the ark to Jerusalem illustrates again the result of polygamy in Old Testament times. Students should consult commentaries as they read these chapters.

THURSDAY

Read chapters 7 and 8. As you read, compare 1 Chronicles 17 and 18. Observe the advice of Nathan on two occasions, as he talks with David concerning the king's desire to build the Temple. Note the promise to build the throne of David. This Davidic covenant tended to take precedence over the Sinai covenant. The prophets called Israel and Judah back to the Sinai covenant. Examine David's prayer in 7:18-29. Note the extent of David's kingdom as pictured in chapter 8. Consult a map for a better understanding. Most scholars believe that chapter 8 is a brief summary of David's conquests, with additional details in chapters 9 and 10.

FRIDAY

Read chapters 9 and 10. It was customary in David's time for a new king to slay all rivals to the throne, so the story of chapter 9 has added interest. Note how David provided care for Jonathan's son. Observe the details of Joab's conquest of Ammon and Syria. Joab was the son of Zeruiah, David's sister, and was a loyal military leader for David all of his public life.

SATURDAY

Read chapters 11 and 12. Note that this marks the beginning of David's downfall. Observe David's sin against Bathsheba in a time when the kings took the law into their own hands. Observe also the way David sent for Uriah, yet feared for him to go home to his wife lest he discover the fact that David was the father of the unborn child. Yet David would have liked for Uriah to go home so that he might suppose he (Uriah) was the father of the child. Uriah was loyal to his fighting men. With what orders did Uriah return to battle? Joab understood the order and reported to David. What did David do when Bathsheba's period of mourning was over? Note verse 27 carefully. What was Nathan's reproof of David? How did David take this reproof? His early punishment? Look for trouble in David's household.

SUNDAY

Review chapters 1-12. Think through the highlights of the story thus far. How did David become king of Judah? Of all Israel? How did he defeat the Philistines and extend his kingdom beyond Palestine? What covenant did God make with David and his seed? How did David reveal a fundamental weakness in character? How was he warned? Observe the fact that David, like Saul, was under judgment by the King of kings.

DETAILED STUDY

Two major ideas stand out in these chapters. The first is the rise of David to power over all Israel, and the second is the sin which almost caused his downfall as king.

A. THE RISE OF DAVID TO POWER OVER ALL ISRAEL.

1. We have already examined David's lament over Saul and Jonathan in chapter 1. Consider the effect of this on Saul's followers.

2. Read chapter 2 for steps in David's rise to power. Note the reported guidance of God in going to Hebron and the enthusiasm with which the men of Judah made David king. What is the appeal of 4b-7, and to whom was this appeal made? How did Joab and Abner carry forward the struggle between the supporters of David and the supporters of Saul?

3. In what ways is this story carried forward in chapter 3? The point of verse 6 is that Abner was about ready to take over the king's harem, and thus to declare himself as the real king. Observe the proposal made by Abner and the requirement placed on him by David. This is a sad blot on David and reveals more of pride than of wisdom. Note how Joab almost spoiled the plan by killing Abner. Read verses 28-39 carefully in this connection.

4. Except for verse 4, chapter 4 marks the next stage in David's rise to power. Evaluate the death of Ishbosheth and David's reaction when the report came to him. What political effect was this designed to have on Saul's supporters? Note that Mephibosheth the son of Jonathan is the remaining claimant to the throne, and he is a cripple. The way is now open for David to become king of all Israel.

5. Note the double story of David's anointing as king over all Israel in 5:1-2 and in 5:3. Consult commentaries on the references to David's years as king over Judah and all Israel. It is significant that David makes Jerusalem rather than Hebron his new capital. Observe the personal and family notes in verses 11-15. These become significant later.

6. In chapter 6, observe how David brought the ark to Jerusalem and established a central shrine for Israel. The curse on Michal reflects the view of that time rather than our own. David the king is now established in Jerusalem.

7. We have already recognized the Davidic covenant associated with chapter 7. Note David's prayer, especially the recognition of God's purpose manifest in Israel's history, and the forward look concerning David's house.

8. As we have already observed, chapters 8 and 10 underscore the extension of David's kingdom, largely through the leadership of Joab. David set up the proper administrative organization to keep his enlarged kingdom under control. The underlying theme of chapters 1-10 is that of the rise of David to power and the extension of his kingdom.

B. David's Sin and Its Consequences.

1. We have already recognized David's tendency to take on additional wives. In 2:2 Ahinoam and Abigail are mentioned as being taken to Hebron. However, in 3:2-5 six wives are mentioned in connection with the naming of certain of David's sons. Note where these wives are from.

2. In 3:12-16 we have noted the sad story of David's insistence that he will not make a covenant with Abner unless Abner brings Michal with him. David's pride rather than Michal's

happiness seems to be foremost in this tragic story. We have already observed the break between David and Michal in 6:16-23. Even though he followed accepted practice of kings in his time, David's weakness is becoming more and more apparent.

3. Note the additional wives mentioned in 5:13. David is moving up in the world, developing a harem like other kings of his day. This also is part of the background of chapters 11 and 12.

4. Observe the setting of chapter 11 in verse 1. Note the imperious way in which David took Bathsheba and later sent her home. When Bathsheba reported the consequences to David, what did he do? It is not completely clear what David had in mind, but apparently it was to have Uriah come home to his wife and later to assume that he (not David) was the child's father. Observe the conversation between David and Uriah, the command given, the failure to obey forthwith, the questions of David, and the reply of Uriah. It is possible that the effort is to make Uriah drunk enough not to be too observant or not to remember what he had done while at home. When this failed, nothing was left for David to do except to take Uriah's life. We have already noted David's command to Joab, carried by Uriah himself, Joab's report to David, and David's taking of Bathsheba after the period of mourning was over.

5. How did Nathan get David to condemn himself in chapter 12? How did Nathan then apply the parable to David? We have observed the pronouncement of judgment from God, David's confession of sin, and the immediate reply of Nathan before he went home. How does this chapter show that David is still responsible to the King of kings?

6. What did David do when the child of Bathsheba became ill? What did he do when the child died? What explanation did he give for taking food now? Some persons believe that David refers to heaven in verse 23, but the Jews rather believed in Sheol, a sphere of almost meaningless existence without personal recognition. (See Alan Richardson, *A Theological Word Book of the Bible,* p. 106.) Observe that the account of the birth of Solomon follows and the favorable view of God upon him. The name Jedediah means "beloved of the Lord."

7. To complete the story of David's responsibility, let us observe that while the covenant of Sinai is not mentioned, the king of Israel is still subject to God. The monarchy is still subject to the theocracy. The prophetic understanding of the priority of the Sinai covenant is well treated in John Bright, *The Kingdom of God,* pp. 45-155. The covenant with David was a covenant with moral responsibility. The Ammonites were defeated, thanks to Joab, but the major weakness of David was within. The consequences of David's sin, as we shall see in the next lesson, were national as well as personal.

C. LESSONS IN LIVING.

Each student must learn his own lesson from this study. We give some as suggestions:

1. The wisdom of David in accomplishing what he believed to be God's will for his life. The study of David's rise to power shows a series of wise acts designed to gain support of all Israel. This is important for us.

2. The importance of developing strong character day by day. David began to play with his weakness and this weakness became more and more of a factor in his life. This is equally true of us. The little sin becomes a big sin and finally throws our whole life into tragedy.

3. God's ability to use persons who are not perfect to accomplish His will. This gives us a place in His Kingdom. Let us seek His will and obey it, but let us not be discouraged when we sin from time to time. He will not cast us off, but will accomplish His purpose through us.

SUGGESTIONS FOR FURTHER READING

A. COMMENTARIES:

The Interpreter's Bible, Vol. 2, pp. 855-875 and 1041-1108.

Kennedy, A. R. S., ed., *The Books of Samuel* (The New Century Bible), Introduction and pp. 197-250.

Kirkpatrick, A. F., *The Second Book of Samuel* (Cambridge Bible), pp. 9-134.

Rust, Eric C., *Judges, Ruth, I and II Samuel* (Layman's Bible Commentary, Vol. 6), pp. 122-138.

Smith, H. F., *The Books of Samuel* (I.C.C.), pp. 265-327.

B. INTRODUCTORY AND BACKGROUND MATERIAL:

Anderson, Bernhard W., *Understanding the Old Testament,* pp. 136-139.
Bright, John, *A History of Israel,* pp. 174-186.
            The Kingdom of God, pp. 35-41.
Napier, B. Davie, *From Faith to Faith,* pp. 128-144.
            Song of the Vineyard, pp. 153-162.
Pfeiffer, Robert H., *Introduction to the Old Testament,* pp. 351-368.

QUESTIONS FOR THOUGHT AND DISCUSSION

1. In view of the customs of earlier times, how ought we to view the acts of David in taking on many wives and building up a harem? Why?

2. Why does the Bible not hide the sins of its heroes? Would we not be better off if we did not know about David's sin? Or is it better to know how God dealt with David and his sin?

3. Do private sins always have public consequences? Why or why not?

4. Can a man become a political leader without compromise? Why or why not?

5. What more than a call is needed for a person to fulfill his vocation? How does one discern a call to a particular vocation?

6. How can and does God speak through the story of 2 Samuel? What does He say to you? How can you help others to hear His voice?

The Rebellion of Absalom and Its Consequences

The problem with which chapters 11 and 12 dealt is now ready to bloom into a national tragedy. It was predicted by Nathan that trouble would arise for David out of his own house. This trouble started with jealousy among the sons of David (by different wives), but ended in an effort by Absalom to usurp the throne occupied by his father. The tragic flight of David and the death of Absalom at the hands of Joab, with further rebellion after David was restored, constitute the major concern of chapters 13-20. As we indicated in the preceding lesson, chapters 21-24 appear to be a miscellaneous collection related to various parts of David's reign. The outline for the entire book is also presented there, and may be reviewed by the student for an over-all view of the book as a whole.

DAILY BIBLE READINGS

MONDAY

Read chapters 13 and 14 carefully. Note the occasion for the trouble between Absalom and Amnon, Absalom's plan of vengeance, his flight to his mother's home in Geshur (2 Samuel 3:3), David's ostracism of Absalom, Joab's efforts to bring him back, and the resentment of Absalom against David. What was Absalom's aim, and what were his methods of gaining a following? Compare 13:38 and 14:28. For how long was Absalom separated from the court of David? This is plenty of time to build up resentment.

TUESDAY

Read chapters 15-17. By what means did Absalom seek to win

favor at the gate of Jerusalem? Note where the conspiracy broke, and David's flight. Observe the double purpose in sending back the ark to Jerusalem. In chapter 16, observe the duplicity of Ziba concerning Mephibosheth, the cursing of David by Shimei, and the conflicting counsel of Ahithophel and Hushai. If we compare 2 Samuel 11:3 and 23:34, we find that Ahithophel was probably Bathsheba's grandfather. He might well have carried a grudge against David. Observe the advice taken and the comment made in 17:14. Note how Hushai warned David, and Ahithophel's suicide. Observe also the calculated politics involved when the Ammonites and Gileadites showed kindness to David.

WEDNESDAY

Read chapters 18 and 19. The forest of Ephraim may have been east of the Jordan in Gilead (so Kirkpatrick, *The Second Book of Samuel,* p. 171), or west of the Jordan in the region of Ephraim (so Rust, Layman's Bible Commentary, Vol. 6, p. 145). The location is uncertain, but that east of the Jordan seems most likely. Observe how David arranged his forces for battle, how Absalom was probably caught by his head in the fork of a tree, how Joab and his men slew Absalom, how the news was brought to David, and how Joab jolted David out of his mourning to assume once again the prerogatives of king. Observe the various persons and groups who now support David as he returns triumphantly to Jerusalem, and David's treatment of each.

THURSDAY

Read chapters 20 and 21. Observe the spirit of rebellion in the kingdom and the steps that were taken to restore order. It is probable that the slaying of the sons of Saul took place soon after his death. The devotion of Rizpah is a striking illustration of a mother's love. See 2 Samuel 9:1-8 concerning Saul's house.

Verse 19 of chapter 21 poses a problem for us if we assume that this is the Goliath slain by David in 1 Samuel 17. Second Chronicles 20:5 states that Elhanan, the son of Jair, slew Lahmi, the brother of Goliath the Gittite. It appears that there were two Goliaths rather than one, that 2 Chronicles 20:5 seeks to correct an earlier text to harmonize these two references, or that a textual error has crept in at some time. We should seek for further light in a reverent spirit.

FRIDAY

Read chapters 22:1—23:7. Psalm 18 should be compared with 22:2-51. A. F. Kirkpatrick assigns both this Psalm and 2 Samuel 22 to David at a period of his greatest prosperity, but William R. Taylor in *The Interpreter's Bible* sees it as two Psalms, and as late post-exilic and pre-exilic dates for the two parts. Whatever the correct date, the song is ascribed to David, and purports to reflect his gratitude. What is his view of God and what is his relation to God? What has God done for him? What reasons does he give for praising God? In chapter 23, what view of God, of righteousness, and of judgment is presented? What do these songs say to you?

SATURDAY

Read chapters 23:8—24:25 and compare 1 Chronicles 21. Observe the mighty men of David, especially those who have already been prominent in the story, such as Abishai, Benaiah, and Asahel. Chapter 24 poses a real problem of interpretation. First Chronicles 21:1 attributes to Satan precisely the same thing here attributed to God, and is regarded by some scholars as an effort to correct the earlier passage in 2 Samuel. In both cases the king acted to override Joab's advice. Some believe that David's sin was pride in his standing army. Observe the size of this army as reported by Joab. Note verse 10, and compare 1 Chronicles 21:7-8. What three kinds of punishment were offered to David? What did he choose? What protest did David make when the death angel came to Jerusalem? Observe David's purchase of the threshing floor of Araunah, and his offering on this site. Solomon's Temple was built on or near this site.

SUNDAY

Review 2 Samuel, especially chapters 13-24. What is your picture of this book as a whole? What does it say concerning David? Concerning God and His providential purpose? What things stand out in your mind at this stage of your study? Be prepared to report these to your study group.

DETAILED STUDY

We propose to examine more carefully the tragic consequences of

David's sin in his own family, and the sustaining power of God even in David's personal and national tragedy. We should remember Nathan's prediction that God would raise up trouble for David out of his own house as a consequence of his sin against Uriah and his taking of Bathsheba from her husband.

A. The Rebellion and Death of Absalom.

1. As you reread chapter 13, note the basic elements in the story: how Amnon devised a scheme to satisfy his infatuation for his half-sister Tamar, how he thrust her from him, how Absalom bided his time for revenge, how David was angry but did not punish Amnon, and how Absalom finally devised a clever scheme for his revenge on Amnon. Then observe the further consequences of Absalom's revenge, not on all of David's sons, but on Amnon only, and his flight to his mother's home in Geshur. This area is directly east of the Sea of Galilee as we know it. Observe also David's longing for Absalom during the three years he was in Geshur. Adultery and murder in David's house demonstrated the fact that his sons had followed their father's example with Bathsheba and Uriah and that much unhappiness followed in its wake. Even though revenge by the nearest of kin was perhaps accepted by tribal custom, it still had tragic consequences.

2. Examine chapter 14 for the steps by which Absalom was returned to his father's presence. Observe that Joab, loyal to David, and understanding the king's sorrow, devised a plan to have the king convict himself. Observe that the king recognized Joab's hand in the matter and sent him to bring Absalom back. However, we cannot but observe the command of verse 24 and the consequences thereof. Was David too unforgiving? Were pressures brought to bear by other sons in David's house? No explanation is given. What reference is made to Absalom and his family? How did Absalom get Joab to intercede for him so that he could be received by his father? Observe the mention of two years in verse 28. Adding these two years to the three years he spent in Geshur, Absalom had five years in which to build up his resentment against David.

3. Chapter 15 describes Absalom's conspiracy and rebellion. Note the stages in his rebellion. *First,* he provided himself with a chariot, horses, and a bodyguard. *Second,* Absalom set out to steal the hearts of the people who came to seek justice. Then at the end of four years (the Hebrew text has forty), Absalom went to Hebron, ostensibly to worship, but with another purpose. How did he seek support for his conspiracy? Observe that Ahithophel, one of David's advisers, joined the conspiracy. What steps did David take when he heard of Absalom's conspiracy? Who went with him? Observe Ittai's loyalty. What reason did David give for sending back the ark to Jerusalem? Note also his purpose to have spies at Absalom's court. What was David's prayer concerning Ahithophel's counsel? Whom did he send to counteract Ahithophel's counsel?

4. Chapters 16 and 17 show how Absalom took possession of the palace and the kingdom as David fled for his life. The greed of Ziba and the desire of loyal Abishai to kill Shimei are maters of human interest, and each has its sequel. Note how Hushai professed loyalty to Absalom and how Ahithophel counseled Absalom to claim his prerogatives as king of Israel. What was Ahithophel's advice concerning the pursuit of David? How did Hushai seek to thwart this advice? How did he get word to David? What did Ahithophel do? Observe where David went to set the battle.

5. Chapter 18, in dramatic fashion, builds up to the death of Absalom. Observe how David, the experienced fighter, groups his forces. Note also his fatherly concern for Absalom. The forest of Ephraim, as we have already noted, appears to have been east of the Jordan, even though the territory associated with the tribe of Ephraim is west of the Jordan. We do not know exactly where the battle was fought. We do know that Absalom's army was routed, that Absalom himself was caught, as *The Interpreter's Bible* suggests, in the fork of a tree. It may be that his hair likewise was entangled. At any rate, Joab and his men killed Absalom and buried him, even though David had urged that Absalom's life be spared. Joab apparently was convinced that Absalom, the traitor and usurper, was better

dead and that the nation would be better off without him alive. After David received news of Absalom's death, what did he do and say? David's sins were coming home to him, for now a second son of the king had met his death.

Personal ambition, lack of filial devotion, and the breakdown of home life, primarily through the polygamous practice of developing a harem in the court, brought their natural fruits in David's family. The life of Uriah may have seemed a small price to pay for satisfying his lust with Bathsheba, but God through the moral universe brought the consequences very much home to David. Does not the experience of David find repetition in the breakdown of family life and of chastity today? And does not God speak to us out of David's experience?

B. GOD'S PROVIDENCE IN SUSTAINING AND RESTORING DAVID.

1. In the story of Ahithophel and Hushai, as well as that of Zadok and Abiathar in chapters 15-17, we have already noted how David received information and foiled the plans of Absalom. We also observed in 15:25-26 David's statement that he was in God's hands. Observe his faith in God's purpose. Note also 16:11-12, where David again expresses confidence that God will do him good.

2. As you read chapter 19 from this point of view, observe both the king's sorrow and Joab's wise suggestion to the king. The situation was difficult for a heartbroken father, but it was also critical for the nation. David must claim the loyalty of those who had gone out to fight for him. Note the description of the confusion that followed Absalom's death, as reported in verses 8b-10, and the proposal contained in the question of verse 10. What suggestion did David make to Zadok and Abiathar concerning the men of Judah? What was their response? Note also the appeal and the promise to Amasa, who had been in Absalom's camp. What did David do when Shimei came seeking forgiveness? What reason did he give for not heeding Abishai's advice? Note how Mephibosheth's story differed from that of Ziba, and David's division of their living. We have already observed what David did to express his gratitude

to Barzillai, who helped to feed his army while he was beyond the Jordan. Note the general rallying to David after Absalom's death. The contest for favor in verses 41-43 and the people who returned to Jerusalem with him indicate clearly that God has sustained him and is restoring him to his kingdom. However, this was not the whole story, as chapter 20 shows.

3. For the other side of the picture, read chapter 20 again, looking this time for problems faced by David. Observe the division of loyalty stated in 20:1-2. On what errand did David send Amasa, the cousin of Joab? How did Joab kill Amasa? Joab at this moment was not technically David's leader, but by the people's choice he regained his place. Observe that after Sheba's revolt had been put down, Joab returned to Jerusalem and the king. David was once again king of all Israel. At this period or at an earlier period in his experience, the thanksgiving recorded in chapter 22 may have been expressed.

4. Examine chapter 22 from this perspective. What is David's view of God? Note how he uses poetic language to picture God coming to him in distress. Observe his professed righteousness in verses 21-25. This would seem to be before his sin against Uriah. Observe David's figures of speech again used to describe God, and the praise of God in verses 47-51. It may be helpful to compare the views expressed in 23:1-7. It is possible that the sentiments of chapter 22 were expressed at more than one period in David's life. While we cannot place this material at a specific period, we may recognize the faith which sustained David in trial, and his understanding of the purpose, the providence, and the power of God in spite of his sin. This is illustrated still further in chapter 24.

5. Note especially 24:10-25. Observe David's confession of sin, which is repeated. Observe also his choice to fall into the hands of God rather than the hands of man (verse 14). He knew the greatness of God's mercy. While we do not know for sure the nature of David's sin in this case, we can recognize his willingness to throw himself on the mercy of God who sustained him.

This study therefore points to the purpose, the mercy, and

the power of God to forgive and to restore David, to sustain and strengthen him in time of trouble. Let us thank God that His saving mercy extends also to us.

C. LESSONS IN LIVING.

Second Samuel 13-24 will speak its own message to each student. We shall suggest and comment upon three significant lessons in living.

1. God usually punishes us through the normal or natural consequences of our sins. This is well illustrated in the experience of David, whose trouble came to him personally and politically "out of his own house." Let us be careful to set only the best example before our children that they may rise up in our example and call us blessed.

2. The greed for power kills. Absalom spun the net in which he was finally killed. We may understand his resentment, but this does not prevent him from bringing his own self-destruction. Nor is this experience limited to Absalom. It is repeated in individual life, in business, in government, in every profession, including those professions associated with full-time church vocations. Let us beware of this subtle lust for power.

3. God always sustains those who truly repent and trust in Him. This truth is written in capital letters in the experience of David. Psalm 51 is the kind of Psalm David might have uttered after he faced his sin, for this is the way he probably felt. God's grace is greater than our sin, but we must not sin that grace may abound. Yet it is wonderful to be able to throw ourselves on God's forgiving mercy, made crystal clear in the gospel of the New Testament.

SUGGESTIONS FOR FURTHER READING

A. COMMENTARIES:

The Interpreter's Bible, Vol. 2, pp. 1108-1176.

Kennedy, A. R. S., ed., *The Books of Samuel* (The New Century Bible), pp. 250-319.

Kirkpatrick, A. F., *The Second Book of Samuel* (Cambridge Bible), pp. 134-241.

Rust, Eric C., *Judges, Ruth, I and II Samuel* (Layman's Bible Commentary, Vol. 6), pp. 138-152.

Smith, H. P., *A Critical and Exegetical Commentary on the Books of Samuel* (I.C.C.), pp. 327-393.

B. INTRODUCTORY AND BACKGROUND MATERIAL:

Anderson, Bernhard W., *Understanding the Old Testament*, pp. 139-143.

Bright, John, *A History of Israel*, pp. 186-189.

          The Kingdom of God, pp. 39-44.

Napier, B. Davie, *Song of the Vineyard*, pp. 162-164.

QUESTIONS FOR THOUGHT AND DISCUSSION

1. What does David's experience teach us about following one's lust and taking another man's wife? Taking another man's life? Do consequences follow our actions as they followed his? Why or why not?

2. What is the difference between ambition and greed? At what point does one stop and the other begin? Why?

3. What is the relation between one's sense of vocation under God and one's desire to serve his fellow men? What part do these play in controlling ambition and preventing greed?

4. Since David sometimes did not seek or did not clearly understand God's will, in what sense is he an example to us? Why?

5. How do you interpret the fact that there is no mention of the Sinai covenant between God and His people in 2 Samuel? Is the kingdom of Israel taking the place of the Kingdom of God? Why do you think as you do?

6. What lessons in living stand out in your mind as a consequence of these studies? How can you help someone else to see them?

The Golden Age
of Solomon

The two books called 1 and 2 Kings in our Bible are actually part of a fourfold book of kings. The division into two books appears in the Septuagint Version of the Old Testament (a translation from the Hebrew into Greek begun about 250 B.C.) as Third and Fourth Kingdoms. In our Bible we refer to them as 1 and 2 Samuel, 1 and 2 Kings. After chapter 11, 2 Kings takes up an account of the reigns of the kings of Israel and Judah, and continues the alternating story until the fall of the kingdom of Israel, which is recorded in 2 Kings 17.

First Kings begins with the problem of throne succession, which had been a live problem since before Absalom's abortive attempt to usurp the throne occupied by his father David. Second Kings moves from Solomon's accession to the glories of his reign and reaches a point of climax in chapter 11. Solomon magnified his father's love for women and built up a tremendous harem, partly for political reasons but also with an undue tolerance of many religious practices forbidden in Israel. The consequence came in the experience of his son and successor, Rehoboam, under whom the kingdom was divided. After chapter 12 the story is one of a divided kingdom. Our concern in this lesson is with the reign of Solomon.

Most scholars propose the following sources for 1 and 2 Kings:

1. The court history of David, which appears to be a continuation of 2 Samuel 9-20 and provides the basic material for 1 Kings 1 and 2.

2. The Book of the Acts of Solomon, referred to in 1 Kings 11:41.

This is believed to have been the basic source for chapters 3-10, with the exception of the song in 1 Kings 8:12-13 and the taunt song in 19:21-28. These two songs are referred to a book of songs or another source. First Kings 11 is believed by many scholars to have been written later, with verses 1a, 3a, 4a, 7-8, as probably coming from the Acts of Solomon.

3. The Book of the Chronicles of the Kings of Israel, frequently referred to, as in 1 Kings 14:19. The author or authors selected material from this source and refer to it as a source in which many other materials are available. The emphasis on Ahab, rather than on Omri and other kings significant in nonbiblical sources, reveals in part the point of view of the writer of 1 Kings. This history probably covered the whole period from Jeroboam I to Hoshea, the last king of Israel. Some suggest that The Acts of Ahab or The History of the Syrian Wars might have provided material for the Ahab-Elijah story. None of these sources is available to modern scholars, so much of this assignment of material becomes precarious unless suggested in the text itself.

4. The Book of the Chronicles of the Kings of Judah, which is referred to in connection with the kings of Judah, just as the other source is used in referring to the history of the kings of Israel. The first reference to this source appears in 1 Kings 14:29. The fact that this book goes to the end of Jehoiakim's reign suggests that it probably was completed soon after that reign was completed.

5. Biographies of the great prophets may have been used as a source for the stories of Elijah, Elisha, Micaiah, and Isaiah. It is believed that the editors not only selected their materials, but also interpreted them in the light of a philosophy of history which is characteristic of what is called the Deuteronomic school. Commentaries will suggest variations in the Hebrew and Septuagint texts. A detailed presentation of sources is given in *The Interpreter's Bible,* Vol. 3, pp. 3-15. Only the major framework is proposed above.

In this survey we will not attempt to deal with the detailed analysis of sources. The date generally assigned for the basic books of 1 and 2 Kings is about 600 B.C. with the Deuteronomic revision about 550 b.c., and with later revisions, mostly under the influence of the Priestly code. Our purpose is to study 1 and 2 Kings in their received form and with a conviction that God inspired the writing which came to us in its final form, using perhaps more than one editor to select, edit, and interpret the materials under the guidance of the Holy Spirit. These books show how God acts in history and what God means to human life. They center primarily in the reigns of the kings of Israel and Judah. We have given attention to these kings in a chart in the next lesson. Let us now recognize the basic outline of chapters 1-11, which are our concern in this lesson.

THE OUTLINE OF CHAPTERS 1-11

General Theme: The Golden Age of Solomon

A. Rivals for David's Throne (ch. 1).
B. Solomon Succeeds David as King (ch. 2).
C. Solomon's Wisdom and Splendor (chs. 3 and 4).
   1. Solomon's wisdom, God's gift (ch. 3).
   2. Solomon's court and splendor (ch. 4).
D. The Building of the Temple (chs. 5-7).
   1. Preparation for building the Temple (ch. 5).
   2. Building the Temple (ch. 6).
   3. Building the palace and Temple furnishings (ch. 7).
E. Dedication of the Temple (ch. 8).
F. Solomon's Glory and Decline (chs. 9-11).
   1. The extension of Solomon's government (ch. 9).
   2. The visit of the Queen of Sheba; Solomon's glory (ch. 10).
   3. Solomon's fading splendor and death (ch. 11).

Please work out your own outline. You will see how the book is organized.

DAILY BIBLE READINGS

Monday

Read chapters 1 and 2. Note the importance of David's successor in his old age. How did Adonijah seek the throne? Who supported Solomon? How did he eliminate his opposition? Note how he secured the throne for himself.

TUESDAY

Read chapter 3. Observe Solomon's important political marriage and his worship at different altars. How was Solomon's prayer for wisdom answered? Keep alert for his sagacity and his tolerance in religious worship.

WEDNESDAY

Read chapters 4 and 5. Who were Solomon's principal officers? How did he organize his kingdom to support his harem? Note the way he cut across tribal boundaries, perhaps to break down tribal loyalties. Observe also how many Israelites (probably from the Northern Kingdom) he put under forced labor. Compare the report in 2 Chronicles 2:17-18. Look for consequences of this practice.

THURSDAY

Read chapters 6 and 7. For a clearer mental picture of the Temple, see *The Westminster Historical Atlas,* revised edition, pp. 48-49; G. Ernest Wright's *Biblical Archaeology,* pp. 136-145; and another version in *Harper's Bible Dictionary,* pp. 732-733. Note who helped in the building, and the amount of time required to build the Temple and Solomon's palace. What is implied about the relative size and importance of each? Note the parallel account in 2 Chronicles 2:13—5:11.

FRIDAY

Read chapter 8. This chapter, which may be revised from its first account, centers in the dedication of the Temple at the Harvest Feast of Ingathering, sometimes called the Feast of Tabernacles or Booths. This feast followed the Feast of Atonement (Yom Kippur), coming about five days later. Observe what is said about David's desire to build the Temple in verses 14-21. Study Solomon's prayer of dedication in verses 22-53. Note also his huge sacrifices.

SATURDAY

Read chapters 9 and 10. Compare 2 Chronicles 9. How is the magnificence of Solomon's kingdom set forth? What did it cost Israel? Observe Solomon's relations with Hiram and the Queen of Sheba. What warning do these chapters give to us concerning self-aggrandizement?

SUNDAY

Read chapter 11. According to verses 1-8, what weakness of David was magnified in Solomon? Observe the series of consequences of false worship in verses 9-13, 14-22, 23-25, and 26-40. Note that Jeroboam is the most dangerous enemy. Observe also the summary statement in verses 41-43 and compare 2 Chronicles 9:29-31, where other historical sources are proposed. What do these chapters teach about the relation between worship and conduct?

DETAILED STUDY

These chapters present in rapid fashion a series of stages in Solomon's reign. We observe first his establishment as king, with a reputation for wisdom given him by God. Second, we note Solomon's building and business interests, which were closely related. Third, we observe the glory and splendor, as well as the slavery, of Solomon's kingdom. Fourth, we note both the true and the false worship of Solomon, which was related to the covenant of God with David, and which had significant consequences. Let us examine these ideas more closely.

A. SOLOMON'S ESTABLISHMENT AS KING.

1. Note in 1 Kings 1:5-10 the purpose of Adonijah, his use of chariots like Absalom in 2 Samuel 15:1, his family connection, his supporters, his court opponents, and his omission of certain men when he went to sacrifice. Examine again the court intrigues by which Solomon's supporters move step by step to have David proclaim Solomon as his successor. How does this reach its climax in the anointing of Solomon by Zadok the priest? What was Jonathan's report to Adonijah? Note what is said about Solomon's throne and David's part in crowning him. What did Adonijah do? What did his followers do? Observe Adonijah's request of Bathsheba, who was probably in charge of the harem, and the fatal consequences of his request.

2. Observe how Abiathar was replaced by Zadok and was sent to perpetual exile in Anathoth, a small town about three miles northeast of Jerusalem. The prophet Jeremiah was one of his more famous descendants.

3. How was Joab slain, and why? Where did he seek protection? Ordinarily this would have provided refuge, but Joab represented a threat to Solomon, or so it seems. Who replaced Joab as the head of Solomon's army?

4. What restriction was placed on Shimei? How and when did he break this restriction? With what result? Note that 2:5-9 points to these consequences for Joab and Shimei. Observe also the summary statement in 2:46b.

5. How does the story of 3:16-28 illustrate the wisdom of Solomon? Observe how this follows Solomon's prayer for wisdom in 3:3-9.

6. Read chapter 4 again carefully, noting the persons and provisions involved in supporting Solomon's court. Observe the two summary statements in verses 20-21 and 29-34.

The establishment of Solomon's kingdom required both clever maneuvering and large provisions. Bathsheba, Zadok the priest, and Benaiah the soldier, joined in the beginning to place him on the throne. Intrigue, bloodshed, and cruelty, such as was common among oriental kings, dissipated any possible organized opposition to his throne. Thus the problem of succession was solved for Solomon. However, the splendor of Solomon's reign came at terrific expense to the people of Israel. This caused unrest which finally broke out at his death and the succession of Rehoboam to the throne.

B. SOLOMON'S BUILDING AND BUSINESS INTERESTS.

The major task of Solomon was to hold together the empire conquered and established by his father David. This was no mean task. The tremendous expense of the court and the ambitious building projects of Solomon had to be underwritten, not only by his own people but also by trade with other countries, by a treaty with Hiram which provided basic materials, by marriage with foreign wives. The local conscription of labor and the draining of Israel's resources were a big price to be paid for the king's ambitions.

1. We have already examined chapter 4, which not only names the chief members of Solomon's court, but also lists the officers who were to provide for Solomon's household one month of each year. Food was provided for persons and also for Solomon's horses each month. Verse 19, which is disputed, suggests also an overseer over Judah. In addition, 5:13-18 reports forced laborers from the kingdom of Israel, and 9:15-22 tells us that these were the Canaanites who dwelt in the land before Israel came, with the Israelites serving as officers over the rest. The amounts suggested in 4:22-28 for Solomon's household are staggering. They were designed to create growing resentment, but apparently Solomon either did not know or did not care what he was doing to the people.

2. Study the treaty or agreement made between Hiram of Tyre and Solomon in chapter 5. Observe the building materials sought by Solomon, the terms of the annual payment, and the plan by which conscripted workmen were sent from Israel to join the workmen from Tyre.

3. The description of building the Temple, as we have noted, is given in chapter 6. We have already suggested additional resources where pictures of reconstructions are provided. Ezekiel 40-43, and especially 41, may be read in this connection. Many scholars believe that the vision of Ezekiel reflects a description of Solomon's Temple. The Phoenician influence was probably pronounced, for the Phoenicians under Hiram had a large part in both the provision of materials and the erection of the building. Note the description and the time required for the building of the Temple.

4. Study again the description of Solomon's palace adjoining the Temple in 7:1-12, and the appointments and vessels for the Temple in the remainder of the chapter. Observe how long was required for building Solomon's palace. Note also verse 8, and the special privilege given to the Pharaoh's daughter.

5. Examine 9:10-14 to see the land sold to Hiram for a hundred

and twenty talents of gold. Hiram apparently got a poor bargain, but Solomon needed money very much.

6. Observe in 9:23-24 the number of chief officers over the building projects of Solomon, and the further reference to the Pharaoh's daughter. Doubtless this marriage helped Solomon to keep the peace with Egypt during this period.

7. Study 9:26-28 and 10:11-29 for the commercial interests and international trade developed by Solomon. We are not certain of the location of Ophir. Southeast Arabia may be the most likely, but note the other suggestions in *The Interpreter's Bible*, Vol. 3, pp. 95-96. Other ports were also visited regularly by the Phoenician fleet. Observe both the precious metals and the other items, and the development of a supply of horses and chariots. Wright's *Biblical Archaeology,* pp. 129-136, gives illustrations of Solomon's palace and stables at Megiddo.

8. In the same article, Wright illustrates the metal mines and smelters which were a further means of support for Solomon's kingdom. From both within and without the nation Solomon used many means of securing income and services for his ambitious program.

C. The Splendor and the Tragedy of Solomon's Kingdom.

This has already been presented in large measure through the description of Solomon's buildings and trade. That Solomon dazzled his contemporaries is well illustrated by the story of the visit of the Queen of Sheba, who may have come to Jerusalem in the interest of mutual trade. Let us study this in greater detail.

1. According to chapter 10, what retinue did the Queen of Sheba bring to Jerusalem? What else? What impressed her most about Solomon's kingdom? How did she express her admiration? What gifts did she bring to Solomon? What did he give her in return?

2. We have already recognized the trade of Solomon, but reread 10:14-22 for a further description of the use of gold and precious materials for Solomon's household. Observe the summary statement in 10:23-25. What gifts are mentioned

here, and how are they related to the glory and splendor of Solomon's kingdom?

3. Against this background, note again 5:13-18 and 9:15-23, and the tragic necessity of slavery to accomplish Solomon's grandiose schemes. We must recognize the fact that slavery was common in ancient times as it is in some parts of the world today. But this was something new, for the Israelites to be slaves to their own king.

We hardly need comment on the "one-man show" of Solomon, grand and glorious to outsiders, but kept up at great expense to the people of Israel. The seeds of discontent finally bore their fruit.

D. SOLOMON'S WORSHIP.

Before and after the dedication of the Temple, Solomon engaged in worship. These experiences provide a very real clue for understanding the success and failure of Solomon as king of Israel.

1. Read 1 Kings 3:3-15 from this point of view. Note the large offering that Solomon was accustomed to offer at Gibeon. What question did the Lord ask Solomon in a dream at night? What was Solomon's admirable answer? Note especially verses 9-14. What promise was made? What condition was set for the added blessing of verse 14? It may be noted in passing that the story in verses 16-28 is an illustration of God's answer to Solomon's prayer for wisdom.

2. The building of the Temple was a preparation for both personal and national worship. The relation to David's purpose is set forth in 5:1-6. Observe that Solomon is carrying forward this purpose in proposing an agreement with Hiram, the king of Tyre. This made possible the building of the Temple for national worship.

3. Reread chapter 8 as a description of worship in magnificent proportions. The ark is probably, but not certainly, the sacred ark brought into the land of Canaan. At least it represents the presence of God to the people. Note especially the words of

verses 12-21. Henceforth until the Exile in 598, 587 B.C., the worship of God ideally is to be centered in Jerusalem. This central place of worship plays a significant role in the thought and life of Israel (and Judah), particularly in the prophetic emphasis on loyalty to the covenant of God with His people Israel. Jeroboam felt it necessary to find substitutes for the worship of God in the Temple when he rebelled against Rehoboam.

4. Solomon's prayer of dedication in verses 22-53 reveals a great deal about the function of the Temple in current and later Judaism. Observe the covenant between God and David's seed (which is taking precedence over the Sinai covenant), underlined in verses 22-26. Note in verses 27-30 that the Temple is to be the place to which the people may turn to pray for forgiveness. Then observe the series of specific instances when men may intercede, such as man's dealings with man in verses 31-32, a time of defeat in battle in verses 33-34, a time of drought in verses 35-36, a time of famine and pestilence in verses 37-40, a prayer of a foreigner in verses 41-43, and a time of fighting in war in verses 44-45. The prayer of verses 46-53 points to the Exile, and is believed to have been added later. However, it contains the same plea for God to hear in heaven and to forgive the people who pray to God toward this place. This is a magnificent and appropriate prayer for the occasion of dedicating the Temple. We have suggested earlier that this was done at the Feast of Ingathering.

5. Note the blessing of Solomon in verses 54-61. The blessing here approaches the traditional understanding of the covenant relationship between God and His people. It is significant in this respect, for the Davidic covenant has been emphasized in 2 Samuel and 1 Kings. The huge offerings made by Solomon (verses 62-64) were probably considered appropriate for this occasion.

6. God's answer to Solomon appears in 9:1-9. Observe the statement in verse 3, which becomes significant for later recorded experiences. Note also the promise of verses 4-5, which relates

to the royal succession to the throne of David. What consequence is threatened if Solomon and his descendants become unfaithful in worship? These verses provide an introduction to the failure of Solomon described in chapter 11.

7. Read 11:1-13 very carefully. What is the warning of verse 2? What consequences followed in verses 3-8? The special favors for the Pharaoh's daughter have already been noted. What punishment is predicted in verses 9-13? The covenant with David concerning the royal line, broken by Solomon, thus comes under the same requirement of faithfulness that the covenant with Israel does. The mercy which allows one tribe (Judah, with Benjamin closely attached) to continue David's line becomes the reason given for only one line in the Southern Kingdom. The three major adversaries of Solomon mentioned are Hadad the Edomite to the south (verses 14-22), Rezon of Damascus to the north (verses 23-25), and Jeroboam the son of Nebat within Israel (who was to receive the ten tribes according to the prophecy of Ahijah, verses 26-40); these provide the outward means by which punishment for his sins was to come upon Solomon. Solomon who lived in glory went out under judgment.

It is not enough to say that this presentation of the downfall of Solomon is Deuteronomic, even though that does appear to be true. For behind the Deuteronomic interpretation of history is the purposive activity of God. This God requires faithfulness in worship and in conduct. This God brings blessing and judgment in the long run, and He brings it usually as the natural consequences of one's attitudes, habits, and practices. Such was the case with Solomon. He had everything his heart could wish, but his heart did not content itself with the wisdom from above. He became unwise in seeking his own glory rather than the glory of God. Solomon still speaks, and the redemptive purpose of God speaks in warning through him.

E. LESSONS IN LIVING.

Each student will draw his own lessons in living from these

chapters. We suggest the following for consideration:

1. The danger of centering the kingdom of Israel in one man. The kingdom of Israel increasingly centered in Solomon, his desires, his wishes, his purposes, his reputation, his glory. This became his downfall. Let every leader who seeks for prestige or power beware! Man's chief end is to glorify God and to enjoy Him for ever.

2. People are more important than buildings. Solomon sowed the seed for his own downfall by exacting demands upon his people for support of his huge harem and court, and by using forced labor for his building projects. Even though this was customary, it was not morally right. Solomon *used* the people instead of *serving* them. The taking of many wives and concubines illustrates again the fact that Solomon's desires were more important than the needs of persons. Churches do well to remember that people are more important than buildings.

3. Worship and conduct either make us or break us. These helped to make Solomon and helped also to break him. Without holding to strict chronology in the arrangement of chapters, we may see how the inspired writer or writers showed how his obedience brought blessings and his disobedience to God brought destruction.

4. God's purpose underlies personal and national (and international) history. The covenant with David's line had its conditions rooted in God's redemptive purpose, just as did the covenant with Israel as a nation. God's purpose is the key to both the Old and the New Testaments. Only in a secondary sense may the covenant relationship be said to provide the basic motif of the Old Testament interpretation of history. How is our life geared to the purpose of God? This is the question that really matters for time and eternity.

SUGGESTIONS FOR FURTHER READING

A. COMMENTARIES:

Barnes, W. E., *The First Book of the Kings* (Cambridge Bible), Introduction and pp. 1-107.

Dentan, Robert C., *I and II Kings, I and II Chronicles* (Layman's Bible Commentary, Vol. 7).

The Interpreter's Bible, Vol. 3, pp. 2-111.

Montgomery, J. A., *A Critical and Exegetical Commentary on the Books of Kings* (I.C.C.), pp. 1-248.

Skinner, John, *Kings* (The New Century Bible), pp. 2-184.

B. INTRODUCTORY AND BACKGROUND MATERIAL:

Anderson, Bernhard W., *Understanding the Old Testament,* pp. 143-153.

Bright, John, *A History of Israel,* pp. 189-208.
          The Kingdom of God, pp. 39-49.

Finegan, Jack, *Light from the Ancient Past,* revised edition, pp. 167-183.

Napier, B. Davie, *Song of the Vineyard,* pp. 164-171.

Pfeiffer, Robert H., *Introduction to the Old Testament,* pp. 374-391.

Wright, G. Ernest, *Biblical Archaeology,* pp. 129-145; abridged edition, pp. 75-89.

Wright, G. Ernest, and Freedman, David M., *The Biblical Archaeologist Reader,* pp. 145-193.

Young, Edward J., *An Introduction to the Old Testament,* pp. 200-205.

QUESTIONS FOR THOUGHT AND DISCUSSION

1. What are the basic elements in Solomon's rise to glory? How are these interpreted in these chapters?

2. How did Solomon magnify both the strength and the weakness of his father David? What traits of character became exaggerated in Solomon's experience?

3. What part does the covenant with David play in the story of chapters 1-11? What were its conditions? How were they related to the conditions of the covenant with all Israel?

4. What is the intimate relation between worship and conduct? How may we develop a higher degree of correlation between our better moments of worship and our total conduct?

5. In what sense does the experience of Solomon become a universal experience? How does his lust for power prove his undoing? How should we interpret his experience?

6. How may we help others to grasp the lessons in living taught by Solomon's experience interpreted in 1 Kings 1-11?

The Divided Kingdom

The tragedy of the divided kingdom cannot be fully explained by the fact that it was never fully a united kingdom. It is true that David faced to the end of his reign certain elements of rebellion and that Solomon further estranged the northern tribes by his forced labor. It is also probably true that there was resentment over the breaking down of the tribal loyalties in the interests of the state. It would therefore be false to assume that the total cause of the division was Rehoboam's rash reply to the men of Israel at his coronation. But this was the occasion of the return of Jeroboam and the request which Rehoboam so unwisely rejected. He had, to be sure, the advice of the young courtiers accustomed to lording it over those who lacked their position.

The roots of Rehoboam's decision lie in the harem and the weakness of character produced (perhaps in large part thereby) in the son of Solomon and the grandson of David. Rehoboam had no adequate home life to serve as a guide in his childhood and youth. Furthermore, because of his father's political and religious tolerance of many gods, he apparently lacked the firm faith in God which would have made him more conscious of his stewardship under God. It is significant that he asked advice from men and not from God, and took the advice of those least able to act wisely.

Concerning sources we refer students to the summary given in the preceding lesson, and to the commentaries and helps proposed for further reading. We will study the finished product which interprets life in the purpose of God.

The over-all picture of the kings of Israel and Judah may be given in the following chart.

THE KINGS AND PROPHETS OF 2 KINGS

Approx. dates B.C.	Kings of Israel	Reference	Kings of Judah	Reference	Prophets
850-849	Ahaziah 2 yrs.	1:1-18			
849-842	Jehoram 12 yrs.	3:1-27; 9:14-26	Jehoram (Joram) 8 yrs.	8:16-24	
851-787					ELISHA
842			Ahaziah 1 yr.	8:25-29; 9:27-28	
842-815	JEHU 28 yrs.	9:1—10:36	Athaliah 6 yrs.	11:1-20	
837-800			Joash 40 yrs.	11:1—13:9	
815-801	Jehoahaz 14 yrs.	13:1-9			
801-786	Joash 16 yrs.	13:10-25; 14:11-16			
800-783			Amaziah 29 yrs.	14:1-22	
786-746	JEROBOAM II 41 yrs.	14:23-39			
783-742			(Azariah) UZZIAH 52 yrs.	15:1-7	
760-747					AMOS
750-735			Jotham 16 yrs.	15:32-38	
746-745	Zechariah	15:8-12			
745	Shallum 1 mo.	15:13-15			
745-738	Menahem 10 yrs.	15:14-22			
738-737	Pekahiah 2 yrs.	15:23-26			
737-732	Pekah 20 yrs.	15:25-31			
735-715			AHAZ	16:1-20	
732-724	Hoshea 9 yrs.	17:1-6			
740-700					ISAIAH 1-39
740-698					MICAH
722-721	FALL OF SAMARIA TO ASSYRIA UNDER SHALMANESER V, SARGON II				
715-687			HEZEKIAH 29 yrs.	18:1—20:21	

Approx. dates B.C.	Kings of Israel	Reference	Kings of Judah	Reference	Prophets
687-642			MANASSEH 55 yrs.	21:1-18	
642-640			Amon 2 yrs.	21:19-26	
640-609			JOSIAH 21 yrs.	22:1—23:30	
627-586					JEREMIAH
614-612					Zephaniah
614-612					Nahum
609			Jehoahaz 3 mos.	23:31-34	
609-598			Jehoiakim 11 yrs.	23:34—24:6	Habakkuk
598-597	First Captivity of Judah		Jehoiachin 3 mos.	24:8-16	
597-587			Zedekiah 11 yrs.	24:17—25:7	
593-571					EZEKIEL
587	FALL OF JERUSALEM TO NEBUCHADNEZZAR OF BABYLONIA				

Several things should be noted about this list of kings. One is that the dates for the kings are those proposed in *The Westminster Historical Atlas,* revised edition, p. 15. These dates are approximate rather than fixed. There are several problems associated with any attempt at a fixed chronology. The years of reign are those suggested in the text, and these do not always harmonize with other dates, primarily because some reigns may overlap, and occasionally because a son serves as regent while his father is still alive.

Concerning the prophets we may observe several who are not listed. These include such persons as Nathan, David's adviser (1:22-40); Ahijah (chs. 11, 14); Shemaiah (12:21-24); Jehu (16:1-7); Micaiah (ch. 22); and later Huldah, the prophetess, in 2 Kings 22. Elijah is the only one included in the chart, and he serves as the counterpart to Ahab of Israel. His dates also are approximate.

As we examine this chart, we may note the following things. *First,* a good deal of space is used to describe the major events of the reigns of Rehoboam and Jeroboam. The events leading to the division of the kingdom serve to highlight the reign of Rehoboam.

The rebellion and the sins of Jeroboam II are given particular emphasis in the account of Jeroboam's reign. *Second,* Omri is highly significant in accounts from other sources, but is given very limited notice in 1 Kings. We have capitalized Omri's name along with others who appear to be outstanding in the life of Israel and Judah. In striking contrast, Ahab and Jezebel claim a large amount of space, serving as the arch rivals of Elijah the prophet. Elijah called the people back to worship God only, and Ahab and Jezebel introduced the worship of the Tyrean Baal (Baal-Melkart) as national policy in Israel. *Third,* Jehoshaphat, like his father Asa, is regarded as a good king because of his reforms in worship in Judah. The recognition of these emphases by time and space relationships in the text gives us a clearer indication of the author's point of view. Loyalty to God and obedience to Him in worship and conduct become the key to the destiny of kings and nations. Further analysis will be encouraged in the daily Bible readings and in the detailed study.

DAILY BIBLE READINGS

Again we remind each student that he must *make* time for study and that he must discipline himself to keep at his work regularly.

MONDAY

Read chapters 12 and 13; compare 2 Chronicles 10:1—11:4; 11: 13-17. Observe the request of the men of Israel, the consultations of Rehoboam, the reply, and the consequences that followed. Why did Rehoboam not attack Israel with his army? What was Jereboam's strategy to prevent the people of Israel from returning to the Temple worship in Jerusalem? The Feast of Ingathering (Harvest) was observed in Israel on the fifteenth day of the eighth month, just one month after the same feast in Judah (see Leviticus 23:39-43). It may be that the crops in the hill country matured later than did those in the valley of the Jordan. Jeroboam's apparent return to Mosaic traditions, however crudely done, may well have had a strong appeal to the Israelites. What do you learn from the experience of Jeroboam at Bethel and from the checkered story of the two prophets? What is said further about Jeroboam?

TUESDAY

Read chapter 14; compare 2 Chronicles 11:5—12:16. Note the plan of Jeroboam to discover what would happen to his sick child. What stern answer did the prophet Ahijah give? With what consequences? How is Jeroboam's reign summarized? Note the formula, referring to the Book of the Chronicles of the Kings of Israel, the length of the king's reign, and his successor. Frequently the bad character of the king is underlined. Very few of the kings of Judah and none of the kings of Israel are praised. This has suggested a southern bias in the present book in favor of the kings of Judah. How is the reign of Rehoboam described? What further details are given in 2 Chronicles? Observe how he followed his father. Note also the grave danger from Egypt. What does chapter 14 say to us from the experience of Jeroboam and Rehoboam?

WEDNESDAY

Read chapters 15 and 16; compare 2 Chronicles 13-16. How is Abijam's reign described? What reforms did Asa make? How is the war between Judah and Israel described? Note the kings involved. How and why was the house of Baasha destroyed? What does 1 Kings say about the reign of Omri? Note the successor to Omri and the evil character of Ahab depicted here. Observe also what is said about his wife Jezebel and her religious background. Bernhard Anderson's *Understanding the Old Testament,* pp. 198-200, and John Bright's *A History of Israel,* pp. 220-223, treat the reign of Omri helpfully.

THURSDAY

Read chapters 17-18. Chapters 17-19 and 21 are really Elijah's story, and are believed to have come from a source depicting the career of this prophet. The great threat to Israel was the worship of Baal-Melkart, the god of the Phoenician nations, particularly of Tyre. This cult and the fertility cult of Canaan, to which it was similar, proved a dangerous threat to the religion of Israel. How does chapter 17 indicate that God is the Lord of the seasons which bring fertility to the land? How does it show that God is Lord of life? How did Elijah return after the three years of famine to announce himself to Ahab? Note the dramatic incident between God and Baal at Mt. Carmel and the prayer of Elijah for rain. What do these chapters say about worshiping the one God instead of the little gods we make for ourselves?

FRIDAY

Read chapters 19 and 21. Note that these chapters complete the story of Elijah's contest with Ahab. How did Jezebel threaten Elijah's life after he had slain the prophets of Baal (probably with some help)? Where did he go and what did God teach him there? How did Jezebel get Naboth's vineyard for Ahab? What message did Elijah bring to Ahab when he went to possess it? Observe the conduct that grows out of the worship of Baal.

SATURDAY

Read chapter 20. Study the first campaign of Ben-hadad of Syria against Ahab in Samaria. How was Ahab delivered? How did the spring campaign in the valley go? How did Ben-hadad escape with his life after being defeated in battle? Note how Ahab was warned by the prophet of God, and how he felt about this rebuke. What does this chapter teach us?

SUNDAY

Read chapter 22; compare 2 Chronicles 17-20. What proposal did the king of Israel make to Jehoshaphat? Note Jehoshaphat's counter proposal. How did the message of Micaiah the prophet differ from the message of the professional prophets? What was the result of the battle at Ramoth-gilead? Note the summary of Ahab's reign. What further details are given concerning Jehoshaphat's reign? Observe how much space is given to him in 2 Chronicles. Who succeeded Jehoshaphat? Who succeeded Ahab? Think through this part of 1 Kings. What does it say to you? Be prepared to share your best findings with your study group.

DETAILED STUDY

In our detailed study we propose to examine more carefully the division and establishment of Israel and Judah, the early wars between Israel and Judah, the contest between Elijah and Ahab-Jezebel as representatives of God and Melkart, and the wars with Syria.

A. The Division and Establishment of Israel and Judah.
Chs. 12-14.

In our previous lesson we recognized the seeds of division sown by Solomon. The failure of David to establish and maintain a unified kingdom without dissenting groups, particularly in the north; the luxurious tastes of Solomon and the expense of his larger court and greatly increased harem; the ornate buildings erected partly through forced labor from the people of the north, usually referred to as Israel; and the centralization of worship and government in Jerusalem and Solomon's toleration of false worship—probably all of these played a significant part in fostering the seeds of discontent. Solomon's effort to kill Jeroboam, who was encouraged by Ahijah to lead ten tribes against the house of Solomon (11:29-40), did not help matters in the least. Jeroboam was sent for and became the spokesman for the people descended from the northern tribes.

1. In chapter 12, note where Rehoboam came to meet with the people of Israel and to be crowned as their king. Apparently he had already been crowned as king over Judah in Jerusalem. What condition is laid down by Jeroboam if the northern tribes are to accept Rehoboam as king? What advice did the older men give Rehoboam? What advice did the young men who had grown up in the court with Rehoboam give him? What was the spirit and what were the words of Rehoboam's answer after three days? Note the interpretation after the event in verse 15. What was the reaction of Israel to Jeroboam's harsh words? Note what was left to Rehoboam. Who was sent to continue the forced labor in Israel? With what result? Note how Rehoboam and Judah reacted.

2. According to verses 21-24, what purpose was in the mind of Rehoboam? Who advised against trying to bring the rebellious Israelites into submission? What reason was given? Observe the fact that this makes the break complete. Thus Judah (with the major portion of Benjamin) became the kingdom of Judah.

3. Examine 14:21-31 for the remainder of Rehoboam's story.

How is Rehoboam identified? For how long did he reign in Jerusalem? With what specific sins is his administration charged in verses 22-24? What did Rehoboam have to pay Shishak of Egypt? Note that the glories of Solomon became the thorn of Rehoboam. Shishak's inscription indicates that he overran a good portion of both Judah and Israel and proved a serious threat to Rehoboam. He did not return with his armies, but exacted heavy tribute, as this passage indicates. His continual war with Jeroboam was probably kept to a slow walk because of danger from the south. Additional material in 2 Chronicles 10-12 may be consulted at this point. Unfortunately we do not have a copy of the Books of the Chronicles of the Kings of Judah and of Israel, to which frequent reference is made in 1 Kings.

From the information given us, we may conclude that the spoiled young prince from the court not only lacked sound judgment, but that he was ambitious to carry forward, at still greater expense to the people, his father's luxurious living. He divided the kingdom permanently and brought it to serious subjugation to Egypt for a time. The moral consequences of both his heritage and his own unfaithfulness to God fashioned his destiny.

4. In the story of Jeroboam in 12:25—14:20, observe the strategy by which Jeroboam estranged the people of Israel from Jerusalem both in political loyalty and in religious worship. Shechem was made the capital, Penuel was built, Bethel and Dan were made centers of worship (locate on a map), high places were erected, priests were appointed (not of the Levites), and a special feast day on the fifteenth day of the eighth month rather than the traditional fifteenth day of the seventh month observed in Judah was appointed. This was the Feast of Ingathering of the Harvest.

5. What message did Jeroboam receive when he was about to sacrifice on the altar at Bethel during the celebration of this feast? From whom and by whom? Note the references to Josiah. It is not certain whether or not this is the king by the same name who reigned in Judah in 640-609 B.C., about three

hundred years after Jeroboam. See *The Interpreter's Bible,* Vol. 3, p. 120, for comments on verses 2 and 3 of chapter 13. It may be helpful to compare Amos 7:10-17; 9:1-10, for a later message at Bethel. What sign was proposed by the man of God concerning the altar? Note verse 5. What happened to Jeroboam? How was his hand restored? Observe why the man of God from Judah did not accept the king's reward and hospitality. Where did he go?

6. We might wish that the story of this courageous but unnamed prophet had stopped at this point. We have already recognized the two prophets and the consequences of an incomplete obedience.

7. What further things did Jeroboam do to provoke God to anger? What consequences followed? What was the message of Ahijah the prophet to Jeroboam through his wife in chapter 14? This appears to be the same Ahijah who prophesied that Jeroboam would become king of Israel in 11:29-40. Note that the requirements of God for the king remain the same, but Jeroboam has failed to obey God's requirements. Note also that the child died as predicted and that the summary of Jeroboam's reign is anything but flattering.

The dark picture of Jeroboam and the other kings of Israel may be attributed in part to the belief that this material comes out of Judah rather than Israel. The prejudice against Israel may show. But having recognized this strong probability, we must remember that Rehoboam came under similar censure. The final question is not where the material was written, but whether or not these kings were faithful to God in worship, conduct, and leadership. Under this requirement they were found wanting. This is more than a Deuteronomic interpretation of history; it is God's view of history deeply embedded in the whole of the Scriptures. The purpose of the Almighty is the key to history.

B. EARLY WARS BETWEEN ISRAEL AND JUDAH. Chs. 15 and 16.

The threat from Egypt appears not to have lasted beyond the reign of Rehoboam, but the reference in 2 Chronicles 14:9-14 to

Zerah, the Ethiopian, indicates a temporary threat to Asa. If modern history provides any kind of parallel, border skirmishes from time to time with a view toward capturing some key town were the type of warfare indicated between Rehoboam and Abijam of Judah and Jeroboam of Israel. More pronounced efforts were made against the Syrians, who were becoming stronger under Ben-hadad of Damascus.

1. Read 15:1-8 for the summary of the reign of Abijam in Judah. What kind of sins did he practice? Why was the kingdom not taken from him? Note how David is held up as an ideal king.

2. How is Asa identified? Compare 15:2 and 15:10, but note also 15:8. It has been proposed that Asa was Abijam's brother; or that the two mothers had a common name and that the phrase "the daughter of Abisholam" was added later; or that Maacah was Asa's grandmother and/or that Maacah continued as head of the harem while Asa was very young, and until Asa removed her because of her idolatries. The latter view seems to make more sense, but we cannot be certain it is correct. What religious reforms did Asa accomplish? Note the thoroughness with which he did things. "Asa did what was right in the eyes of the Lord." This is the highest commendation that can be given to one of the kings.

3. Asa, however, was less astute in his wars with Baasha the king of Israel, at least according to 2 Chronicles 16:7-10. As you read 1 Kings 15:16-24, remember that Ramah was approximately five miles north of Jerusalem, so Asa's situation was grave. How did Asa bribe Ben-hadad to break his agreement with Baasha? With what result? Note that the towns of verse 20 are to the north of Israel and probably served as border towns. Baasha was removed to Tirzah, probably about five miles northeast of Shechem and at least thirty miles from Ramah. The location of Tirzah awaits further confirmation. Note what Asa did when Baasha moved northward. Geba and Mizpeh flanked Ramah on either side. It is helpful to locate these places on a map. Note what is said about Asa's disease late in his life.

Two things stand out in Asa's reign. One is his religious zeal which led to drastic reforms in worship. The other is his political action by which he secured release from Baasha by bribing Ben-hadad I of Syria. He is censured in 2 Chronicles 16:7-10, but not in Kings, for this latter act.

4. Note the brief summary of Nadab's reign of two years in Israel in 15:25-32, and the fact that Baasha killed the whole house of Jeroboam. This is viewed by the inspired writer as a judgment of God upon his house, and it is a fulfillment of Ahijah's prediction in 14:7-16.

5. Examine the character of Baasha's reign, and the prediction of Jehu concerning his house. Note how roundly Baasha's reign is scored.

6. The account of Omri's reign in 16:17-28 does not indicate civil war with Judah. Under Ahab and Jehoshaphat the greater danger came from Syria, so we turn our attention to the threat from that nation.

C. THE WARS WITH SYRIA. Chs. 20, 22.

In chapter 16 we found Asa, king of Judah, bribing Ben-hadad, king of Syria, to attack the Northern Kingdom during his reign. John Bright suggests that the Ben-hadad of chapter 20 is the same king (*A History of Israel,* pp. 221, 224, footnotes). Whether he was the same person or a son and successor, the Ben-hadad of chapter 20 was a formidable enemy of Israel.

1. According to chapter 20, how many kings joined Ben-hadad in his siege of Samaria? These were petty kings, probably in most cases like mayors of modern towns or cities. What was Ben-hadad's first reported demand of Ahab? What was Ahab's reply? What was Ben-hadad's second message? What was the advice of the elders of Israel? Note the further reply of Ben-hadad and Ahab's further reply in verse 11. What instructions were given to Ahab by a prophet of God? How did this plan work out? What further warning did the prophet give to Ahab?

2. By what reasoning did the Syrians pitch the battle in the plain at Aphek near the Mediterranean coast? Note the message given by a prophet to the king of Israel. By what strategy

did Ben-hadad save his life? We have already observed that a son of the prophets criticized Ahab and made him angry for not killing Ben-hadad.

3. Chapter 22 continues the story of the conflict with Syria. It appears that Ramoth-gilead, east of the Jordan, was now in Syrian hands. Observe that Ahab took the initiative and that Jehoshaphat of Judah was more cautious, seeking further guidance. What did the prophets of Ahab say? Who was not present? How did Ahab describe him? Note Micaiah's first message to Ahab, which appears to be an ironic criticism of the other prophets. Observe his second more serious warning to Ahab, Zedekiah's question, Micaiah's reply, and Ahab's sentence upon Micaiah. Micaiah stands out as one willing to pay with his life for speaking fearlessly in the name of God. This requirement of prophetic speaking is still with us.

4. How did Jehoshaphat escape in battle? How was Ahab killed? Note the reference to the fulfillment of prophecy concerning Ahab. How is his reign summarized, and who was his successor? Note the two summaries in verses 41-50 and 51-53.

It is clear that while there was no further immediate danger from Egypt, the Aramean kingdom of Syria posed a serious threat to both Judah and Israel during the reigns of Ahab and Jehoshaphat. Late in his reign, following the battle reported in chapter 20, Ahab joined with a coalition of states led by Ben-hadad of Syria against the onslaughts of Shalmaneser III, and helped to stop this king at the battle of Qarqar in 853 b.c. Our knowledge of this battle, to which Ahab contributed two thousand chariots and ten thousand foot soldiers, comes from Shalmaneser's inscriptions, a copy of which may be read in James Pritchard's *Near Eastern Studies,* pp. 278-279. The danger from without was in direct proportion to the weakness within, but was accentuated by the strength or weakness of Israel and Judah's neighbors to the north and to the south. This inner weakness is best illustrated by the story of Elijah and Ahab-Jezebel, to which we now turn our attention.

D. THE STRUGGLE BETWEEN ELIJAH AND AHAB-JEZEBEL.

We shall do well to remember that the Baal worship brought to Israel through Ahab and Jezebel was the counterpart of the fertility cult of the Canaanites, featuring the god of rain and crops, and affording sensual practices. Jezebel imported Tyrean priests and made Baal worship common among the Israelites. *Harper's Bible Dictionary,* p. 89; James B. Pritchard's *Archaeology and the Bible,* pp. 106-126; and Wright's *Biblical Archaeology,* pp. 98-119, treat the threats to Israel's worship.

1. Read chapter 17 against the background of 16:29-34. Note how Ahab and Jezebel sought to make Baal worship normative for Israel, using this worship as the key to rain, fertile land, and fertile people. Observe Elijah's words to Ahab in verse 1. How was Elijah kept alive at Cherith and at Zarephath? Note the location of Zarephath. God was the God of life as well as the God of food.

2. Chapter 18 describes the dramatic struggle between Ahab-Jezebel and their god and Elijah and the God of Israel. How did Elijah find Ahab? What proposal did he make? Note the number of Baal prophets supported by Jezebel.

3. What choice did Elijah propose on Mt. Carmel? Study the details of the test, the effort to call down fire from heaven, Elijah's prayer, and God's answer. How did God vindicate Elijah's faith? What did this say to Israel? Where did Ahab and Elijah go?

4. Where did Elijah flee when he was threatened by Jezebel after slaying the prophets of Baal? Observe that Beersheba is about fifty miles southwest of Jerusalem and about a hundred miles from Samaria. Note that he made his way to the wilderness of Sinai, with its rich associations. Study the reported conversation between Elijah and God, and the command given to Elijah. Observe the number of Israelites who have not succumbed to Baal worship, and the call of Elisha as Elijah's successor. God will carry on His purpose.

5. Examine chapter 21 carefully. Note the ruthless way that Ahab and Jezebel dealt with Naboth, who counted his land

a sacred trust from God. What did Jezebel say to her pouting husband when she killed Naboth? What warning did Elijah give to Naboth when he went to claim the vineyard? Look for the way this works out in your further study. Observe the comment of the inspired writer in 22:37-40 after the judgment came. The God of Israel is much stronger than Baal-Melkart. Ahab and Jezebel were judged for misconduct as well as false worship. The purpose of God will surely be accomplished in the long run. Let men obey Him!

E. LESSONS IN LIVING.

1. No nation is strong which builds on the suffering of its people. This is especially true when this suffering does violence to human personality and human life. The suffering which is voluntary and for a purpose may help make the nation strong.

2. Danger from without the nation is in proportion to the weakness within. The weak nation but awaits the threat of a strong nation without.

3. The character of a people is fashioned by the quality of its worship. Take Ahab-Jezebel as an example.

4. Moments of great courage may be followed by moments of weakness. Elijah serves as a case in point.

5. God's purpose is the final key to the destiny of individuals and nations. We do well to remember that this is true.

SUGGESTIONS FOR FURTHER READING

A. COMMENTARIES:

Barnes, W. E., *The First Book of the Kings* (Cambridge Bible), pp. 108-182.

Dentan, Robert C., *I and II Kings, I and II Chronicles* (Layman's Bible Commentary, Vol. 7).

The Interpreter's Bible, Vol. 3, pp. 111-186.

Montgomery, J. A., and Gehman, H. S., *A Critical and Exegetical Commentary on the Books of Kings* (I.C.C.), pp. 248-348.

Robinson, Gordon, *Historians of Israel* (I), pp. 65-70.

Skinner, John, *Kings* (The New Century Bible), pp. 184-271.

B. INTRODUCTORY AND BACKGROUND MATERIAL:

Anderson, Bernhard W., *Understanding the Old Testament,* pp. 188-213.

Bright, John, *A History of Israel,* pp. 209-228.

The Kingdom of God, pp. 49-54.

Finegan, Jack, *Light from the Ancient Past,* revised edition, pp. 171, 183-189.

Napier, B. Davie, *From Faith to Faith,* pp. 144-155.

Song of the Vineyard, pp. 172-195.

Pfeiffer, Robert H., *Introduction to the Old Testament,* pp. 391-406.

Pritchard, James B., *Archaeology and the Old Testament,* pp. 91-126.

The Westminster Historical Atlas, revised edition, pp. 50-53.

Wright, G. Ernest, *Biblical Archaeology,* pp. 146-156; abridged edition, pp. 90-97.

Young, Edward J., *An Introduction to the Old Testament,* pp. 205-209.

QUESTIONS FOR THOUGHT AND DISCUSSION

1. What major lesson does Rehoboam teach us? In what sense does our personal faith find expression in our outward conduct? Our decisions?
2. What does Jeroboam say to us about the responsibility of political leadership? Religious faithfulness?
3. How is our culture constantly struggling against non-Christian influences? What are some of these influences? How are they like or unlike those to which some kings and many of the people in Israel and Judah succumbed?
4. What lessons in living do you learn from Ahab and Jezebel?
5. What does Elijah say to us today? What strengths and weaknesses does he reveal?
6. How would you help others to see the major lessons taught in these chapters?

The Dark Days of Israel and Judah

Second Kings has a time span from about 845 to 587 B.C., which is a period of two hundred and sixty years. If we can imagine the history of the United States from the early 1700's to the present, we can grasp something of the period covered. But who can write on thirty-three pages the story of the presidents of the United States during that time? The task of the inspired writer or writers who brought 2 Kings into its present form may be conceived by this comparison. The difference is that for almost half of the time the writer of 2 Kings had two kingdoms to write about instead of one, making the comparison equal to the time from the settlement of Jamestown in 1607 to the present.

The material, which may at first seem to be without order, turns out to fit a pattern well conceived and a message clearly taught in the book itself. The major sources for 2 Kings are believed to be the Books of the Chronicles of the Kings of Israel and Judah. These are not to be confused with 1 and 2 Chronicles in our Bible. The stories of Elisha form the basis for a part of 2:1—9:13. Norman Snaith in *The Interpreter's Bible,* Vol. 3, pp. 4-15, discusses the probable sources of this book and of 1 Kings. He describes tales from the north, of which these earlier chapters in 2 Kings are a part; and tales of the south, particularly 2 Kings 18:13—20:19, in his analysis of sources. He also proposes two Deuteronomic editors, one about 610 B.C. and another about 550 B.C. who brought the material into its final form, and gave it, for the most part, its prophetic or Deuteronomic interpretation. Chapter 17:7-20, 34-41, serves as a good example of this interpretation of history. We suggest that the student examine carefully the analysis made in critical commentaries but remember that our purpose in this survey is to study the content and the message of the book in its final form.

Approx. dates B.C.	Kings of Israel	Reference	Kings of Judah	Reference	Prophets
1020-1000	SAUL	1 Samuel			
1000-961	DAVID	2 Samuel			
961-922	SOLOMON	1 Kings 1:1—11:43			
DIVISION OF KINGDOM					
922-901	JEROBOAM I 22 yrs.	1 Kings 12:25—14:20	REHOBOAM 17 yrs.	12:1-24; 14:21-31	
915-913			Abijam 3 yrs.	15:1-8	
913-873			Asa 41 yrs.	15:9-24	
901-900	Nadab 2 yrs.	15:25-26			
900-877	Baasha 24 yrs.	15:27—16:7			
877-876	Elah 2 yrs.	16:8			
876	Zimri 7 days	16:9-20			
876-869	OMRI 12 yrs.	16:21-28			
873-849			JEHOSHAPHAT 25 yrs.	22:1-50	
869-850	AHAB 22 yrs.	16:29—22:40; 17:1—21:29			ELIJAH vs. Ahab c. 871-850
850-849	Ahaziah 2 yrs.	2 Kings 22:51-53			

The kings and prophets of 2 Kings will be given in the next lesson.

The dates proposed above are those of *The Westminster Historical Atlas*, p. 15, and the number of years for kings are those in the text of 2 Kings. These do not always coincide. Note especially the dates for Jotham, who probably reigned for a time as co-regent with his leprous father, and for Pekah, where again the years do not coincide. Consult commentaries on these problems. We have suggested the dates for the prophets. Jonah is the most disputed as to date, the range being from 600-200 b.c.

B.C.	
587-538 or later	Second Isaiah 40-66
538	Return of the Remnant to Jerusalem under Zerubbabel
520	Haggai
520-519	Zechariah
457 or later	Return under Ezra
450	Malachi
445	First return of Nehemiah
422	Second return of Nehemiah
400-350	Joel
600-200	Jonah
587-400	Obadiah
331	Alexander the Great takes Palestine from Persian control
168-164	Daniel

Now let us turn our attention to 2 Kings 1-10, using the daily Bible readings as a means of grasping the material.

DAILY BIBLE READINGS

Monday

Read 2 Kings 1 and 2. Study the reason for sending a message for Elijah, his reply, and the repetition of this message in person. By what steps did Elisha remain with Elijah, hoping to receive the promise of a double portion of his spirit? *The Interpreter's Bible,* Volume 3, p. 188, on the Gilgal north of Bethel, mentioned in 2:1. Do you think the stories of Elisha are exaggerated? Why?

Tuesday

Read chapters 3 and 4. How is Jehoram's reign described? What three kings went against the king of Moab? How did they win the victory, and how did the king of Moab win a final victory? The Moabite Stone reports that the king of Moab regained the territory of Moab. Note the continued reference to the miraculous power given to Elisha.

WEDNESDAY

Read chapters 5:1—6:23. Examine the story of Naaman and Elisha, the command given to Naaman, and the result when he obeyed. Observe the disastrous consequence of Gehazi's seeking the gifts which Elisha had refused. How did Elisha make an axehead float? How was Elisha delivered from the king of Syria?

THURSDAY

Read 6:24—7:20. How severe was the famine during the siege of Samaria, as the people were being starved into submission? What was Elisha's message to the elders? To the king? How did four lepers help to bring Elisha's prediction to pass?

FRIDAY

Read chapters 8 and 9. How did the Shunammite woman receive her land again? What was Elisha's reply to the king of Syria? Note the description of the efforts of Joram of Israel and Ahaziah of Judah to hold off Hazael of Syria. Who anointed Jehu? How did he purge the house of Ahab? Note the bloody way in which he acted.

SATURDAY

Read chapter 10. How did Jehu secure the death of Ahab's sons? Note his claim of innocence. What did he do to the kinsmen of Ahaziah? Remember that Athaliah was the daughter of Ahab (2 Kings 8:18). Note that Jehu claimed friendship with Jonadab. Observe how he slew the prophets, priests, and worshipers of Baal. How is Jehu's reign summarized? How were the borders of Israel gradually reduced?

SUNDAY

Review chapters 1-10. Think through the stories of Elisha, the wars with Syria and other nations, and the bloody judgments of Jehu. In the long view of history, looking back over these events, how is God's purpose worked out?

DETAILED STUDY

We wish to underscore three things in this part of our study. One is the power given to Elisha, another is Jehu's destruction of the house of Ahab (Omri), and a third is the decimation of Israel and Judah by their neighbors.

A. The Power Given to Elisha.

1. Note the two things in Elisha's mind as he follows Elijah from Gilgal to Bethel to Jericho. As chapter 2 indicates, Elisha knew that Elijah would depart and he would not leave Elijah. After Elijah had smitten the Jordan and had passed over in the presence of a school of the prophets, what request did Elisha make of him? On what condition was this request to be granted? How did Elijah fade from his view? Some scholars take the idea of Elijah's going up in a whirlwind literally, and others regard this as a most fitting poetic way of describing his death. It is clear that the inspired writer wished to convey the idea that Elijah left this life by extraordinary rather than ordinary means.

2. After Elisha had indicated his act of mourning by tearing his clothes in two pieces, what did he take up? What did he say when he smote the Jordan? With what result? The power of God was believed to be for a time in this mantle. Observe how the fifty prophets recognized the spirit of Elijah on Elisha. Also notice that the search for Elijah was unsuccessful. How do the two incidents that follow reveal the authority of Elisha and the respect due to him? Note the assumption that the curse of Elisha on the boys and the destruction of forty-two of them by the she-bears from the woods are directly related. The immediate question is, Did Elisha send the bears to attack the boys? Or is this a case of putting two and two together after they were destroyed? The latter seems more likely. To the Jewish mind, what happens is usually regarded as the act of God. We cannot harmonize this with Jesus' teaching on loving our enemies in Matthew 5:44 or with His example in prayer for those who had Him crucified (Luke 23:34), but we are probably unfair if we criticize this passage by the later revealed standards of conduct. Had we lived in Elisha's day, we might have found it teaching an acceptable lesson of respect for a man of God.

3. Chapters 4-7 contain an account of a number of mighty acts

of God through Elisha. Note in 4:1-7 that the poor widow was sustained by the food provided through Elisha. Verses 8-37 center in the Shunammite woman. She was wealthy rather than poor. Observe what she did for Elisha, the promise and birth of a son, and her hurried trip to Elisha when her son died. By what means did Elisha restore life to the boy? Observe the woman's deep gratitude.

4. In 4:38-44, when wild gourds, now called colycyth, were put into the pottage, observe the poison reported. The pulp of the fruit of colycyth is a powerful cathartic and is poisonous in large quantities. Elisha added meal to the pot, thus weakening the poison and making the pottage safe to eat. This was counted a mighty work though not necessarily a miracle.

5. What kind of offering did the man from Baal-shalishah (place uncertain, but perhaps near Mount Carmel) bring to the prophet? How many were fed with this offering, and what was left? Of what New Testament miracle does this remind you?

6. How is Naaman described in chapter 5? Observe how he heard about Elisha. To whom did the king of Syria send a message by Naaman? Note what the king of Israel suspected when he read the letter. However, it was natural for one king to address another. What message did Elisha send to the king of Israel? Observe what Elisha did when Naaman appeared at his door. Why was Naaman angry? What did he finally do when his servants urged him to bathe in the Jordan? With what result?

7. What did Naaman do when he found himself well? Observe what he offered to Elisha, and the request he made of him. Since he had received healing from the waters of Palestine, he might have felt that he would receive blessing and power from the soil of Palestine when he went to worship. People of that day somehow felt that the god and the land were closely united. We have already noted Gehazi's greed and the consequences thereof.

8. What were the sons of the prophets building when one of them lost an axehead? What use did Elisha make of a stick?

Note that the axe was recovered. This story is used often as a whipping boy in the Old Testament miracle stories. Had the author stated that Elisha put a stick in the axe and raised it to the surface of the water, telling the man to pull it to the bank, modern men would think nothing of the incident. But the statement that the axe was made to float sets up a negative attitude of mind which refuses to approach understanding. The God who made the world could make an axe to float. How He did it in this case is not explained, at least not to the satisfaction of many western minds.

9. According to 6:13-14, who was sent to Dothan (about twelve air miles north of Samaria) to apprehend Elisha? How was Elisha protected by God? What did Elisha propose that the king do with these soldiers? With what result for a time?

10. The famine resulting from the siege of Samaria (6:24—7:20) had dire consequences. John Bright (*A History of Israel,* p. 221, footnote) suggests that this was the Ben-haded who was the enemy of Baasha as well as of Ahab. Others refer to him as Ben-hadad III. Eighty shekels for an ass's head would be about $45.00 in our money. The Septuagint has fifty shekels, which would be about $28.00. The fact that two mothers had agreed to eat their children illustrates the terrible nature of the siege. Note how Elisha's predictive powers were vindicated through the discovery and report of the two lepers.

11. According to 8:1-6, who interceded for the Shunammite woman? Observe another great deed by Elisha. Since Gehazi's leprosy is recorded in 5:27, we may guess that some of this material is arranged in logical rather than chronological order.

12. Two other acts of Elisha, the one concerning Hazael as the future king over Syria (8:7-15), and the other concerning the prophet sent by Elisha to anoint Jehu as the new king over Israel (9:1-10), may also be noted as the work of the prophet. Both of these kings were to become instruments of God's judgment.

Several attitudes have been taken toward these accounts of Elisha's mighty acts. Some regard them as Jewish "wonder stories"; others as actual fact; still others as mighty acts of God through the prophet. The latter point of view is closer to the point of view of the Bible as a whole.

Some interpreters regard Elisha as a leader of insurrection against the house of Ahab. *The Interpreter's Bible,* Vol. 3, p. 230, says: "Elisha encouraged Hazael to murder his master Ben-hadad in Damascus (8:13), and now he raises up Jehu to be an enemy within Israel itself." We should be careful not to overstate the role of Elisha and the prophets in evaluating the acts of Hazael and Jehu. Both of them acted in character, and needed little or no encouragement to engage in their selfish acts. Having said this, we would recognize the fact that, because of the false worship for which they stood, the prophets rejoiced in the punishment of the house of Ahab. From their point of view, Jehu was the instrument of God's judgment on the house of Omri.

B. The Wars with Syria and Other Nations.

It appears, that during the reigns of Omri and Ahab over Israel (876-850 b.c.) and of Jehoshaphat over Judah, the political fortunes of both Israel and Judah were greatly improved. Through the marriage of Ahab and Jezebel, an alliance between Israel and Tyre was strengthened. A similar marriage between Athaliah, Ahab's daughter (or sister), to Jehoram, the son of Jehoshaphat, appears to have stopped civil wars and to have made possible a united action against their neighbors. Annual tribute was exacted from Moab by Israel, and the kings of both Judah and Edom went with Jehoram of Israel to bring a recalcitrant Moab into line. Further details will be found in the background material suggested for reading at the end of this lesson. Needless to say, the position of strength for Israel and Judah became one of weakness. Let us note some of the details.

1. After a brief summary of Jehoram's reign over Israel in 2 Kings 3:1-3, what does the writer tell us about Mesha's re-

bellion at Ahab's death? Observe who went with Jehoram of Israel to punish Mesha. We have already recognized Elisha's promise of water for the Israelites and their allies. Observe the conclusion reached by the king of Moab when he saw water as blood early one morning, his sacrifice of his eldest son, and his wrath against Israel. We have already referred to the Moabite Stone, which records a great victory for Moab on this occasion. Trouble to the south without question cut down on the power of Israel and Judah.

2. Even though Elisha had been instrumental in effecting a temporary truce between Israel and Syria (6:23 in larger context), the danger from Syria was a constant threat to Israel and Judah. The story of the famine and deliverance in 6:24—7:20 illustrates dramatically how near Samaria came to falling. Desperate starvation had set in when God miraculously delivered Samaria from the Syrian army. Second Kings 7:6-7 reports the fears which put the Syrian army to flight. The general summary in 10:32-34 shows that Israel lived in a struggle for survival like that against the Philistines during the time of Saul.

3. Now note 8:16-22 carefully, and the fact that Edom successfully won her independence from Judah during the reign of Joram king of Judah. This again underscores the fact that the power of Judah was fading, and that Judah like Israel was struggling for survival.

C. JEHU'S DESTRUCTION OF THE HOUSE OF AHAB.

Ahab, the son of Omri, represents the dynasty of Omri in this story. But since Ahab was married to Jezebel and permitted this strong-willed queen to act in his behalf, bringing in idolatrous Baal-Melkart worship from Tyre and making this worship a state policy, the prediction given through Elijah in 1 Kings 19:15-17 finally found expression and fulfillment in the account of 2 Kings 9 and 10.

1. Observe the instruction given concerning Jehu to one of the prophets in chapter 9. Observe what the young prophet was

to do as soon as he anointed Jehu, and the details of the message to be given to him. Observe also how the prophet anointed Jehu at Ramoth-gilead beyond the Jordan, delivered his message, and fled. How was Jehu accepted by his followers? After Jehu had warned his men and besought their silence, he set out to kill Joram.

2. Note that Ahaziah, the king of Judah, was visiting Joram while he was being healed of his wounds in Jezreel. Observe Jehu's approach to Jezreel. What did he tell the first two horsemen to do? How was Jehu's riding described? Where did the kings, Joram and Ahaziah, meet Jehu? Note Jehu's answer to the inquiry, "Is it peace, Jehu?" After Jehu had shot an arrow into the heart of Joram, what did he command his aide to do? Note the dramatic justice of this act. What was done with Ahaziah the king of Judah? He was of the seed of Ahab through Athaliah his mother. Where did Ahaziah die, and where was he buried?

3. The death of Jezebel is fitting to her character. How is she described as she looked out of a window? How did she address Jehu? We recall that Zimri had killed Elah, the son of Baasha, and had temporarily taken his throne. Who assisted in Jezebel's death? How was she killed? Note that Jehu was willing to give Jezebel a decent burial after killing her mercilessly. This may be merely an introduction to the words of verses 36 and 37.

4. What was Jehu's first letter to the elders and guardians of the sons of Ahab in Samaria? Note the challenge to crown a king and fight for him. Observe their meek reply. What further condition did Jehu set in his second letter? What did the men of Samaria do? Note how Jehu gave God credit for slaying the house of Ahab, but he himself finished off a few more friends and priests of the house of Ahab. What did Jehu do to the forty-two kinsmen of Ahaziah who were on the way to visit the princes of Israel?

5. By what ruse did Jehu assemble all of the prophets and priests of Baal? Note how he called for the vestments of worship. What command did he give to the worshipers of Baal? What

command had he given to his eighty men? How did they destroy the worshipers of Baal? What else did they do?

6. Study the summary of Jehu's reign in verses 28-36. Note that he destroyed the organized worship of Baal-Melkart, brought into Israel through Ahab and Jezebel, but that he also failed to obey the God of Israel. He followed in the sins of Jeroboam, the son of Nebat, who made Israel to sin. Jehu needed more than strong feeling against Ahab's family and the worship of Baal-Melkart to render his finest possible service.

The book of 2 Kings heartily approves the destruction of the house of Ahab and all it stood for. At the same time it does not approve the false worship of God through the golden calves. Canaanite influence could be as deadly as the Phoenician to the spiritual life of Israel.

D. LESSONS IN LIVING.

1. Personal religion has a tremendous influence on national policy. The character of the leaders determined their policies.
2. Personal religion affects relations with other nations. The strength or weakness of Israel and Judah was in direct proportion to their faithfulness to God.
3. The power of God stands out strongly during the dark days of Israel's weakness. Elisha is a symbol of this power.
4. History is the story of God's moral action. This is not an arbitrary or vindictive activity of God. It is an expression of God's redemptive purpose which uses alike the power of Elisha and the bloody acts of judgment through Jehu.
5. Develop your own lessons in living. Let each part of the Scriptures speak directly to your need.

SUGGESTIONS FOR FURTHER READING

A. COMMENTARIES:

Barnes, W. E., *The Second Book of the Kings* (Cambridge Bible), Introduction and pp. 1-53.
Dentan, Robert C., *I and II Kings, I and II Chronicles* (Layman's Bible Commentary, Vol. 7).
The Interpreter's Bible, Vol. 3, pp. 187-244.

Montgomery, J. A., *A Critical and Exegetical Commentary on the Books of Kings* (I.C.C.), pp. 348-416.
Robinson, Gordon, *Historians of Israel* (1), pp. 70-72.
Skinner, John, *Kings* (The New Century Bible), Introduction and pp. 272-335.

B. INTRODUCTORY AND BACKGROUND MATERIAL:

Anderson, Bernhard W., *Understanding the Old Testament*, pp. 213-222.
Bright, John, *A History of Israel*, pp. 228-234.
          The Kingdom of God, pp. 54-58.
Pfeiffer, Robert H., *Introduction to the Old Testament*, pp. 406-412.
The Westminster Historical Atlas, revised edition, pp. 53-54.
Wright, G. Ernest, *Biblical Archaeology*, pp. 106-119, 151-160; abridged edition, pp. 94-102.

QUESTIONS FOR THOUGHT AND DISCUSSION

1. How do you interpret the Elisha stories? How much do you allow for the thought forms of the Hebrew people in ancient times, and how much do you understand literally? Why?

2. Does God perform miracles today? Why or why not? How does God work?

3. Does God use one individual or one nation to punish another? Why or why not? How does God work in history to accomplish His purpose?

4. If we had only 2 Kings 1-10 as our Bible, what view of God would we hold? How is this book supplemented by other books, including those of the New Testament?

5. What are the strongest things these chapters say to you? How can you help others to see what you have seen in your study?

The Last Days of Israel

From the death of Jehu to the Assyrian captivity one king stands out above all others for his strength and wickedness. This is Jeroboam II, whose reign, as indicated in the chart in the preceding lesson, was from 786-746 B.C. This was also the period which gave to Israel her final "softness" of character and religion and gave rise to a succession of prophets, the first of whom was Amos. He was followed by Hosea, Isaiah, and Micah. The significant date toward which history was moving is 722/721 B.C., for in that fateful year Samaria, the capital of Israel, fell after a terrible siege. However, the series of vassal kings and the murders served as straws in the wind pointing to this fateful tragedy.

The reforms under Joash in Judah and the significant reigns of Uzziah (Azariah), Ahaz, and Hezekiah mark the bright spots in Judah up to and beyond the fall of Samaria. These kings and others are listed in the chart in the preceding lesson, and should be reviewed at this point.

The material of these chapters comes mostly from the Chronicles of the Kings of Israel and Judah. The interpretation of history is strongly prophetic or Deuteronomic.

DAILY BIBLE READINGS

MONDAY

Read chapters 11 and 12. What did Athaliah do to secure the throne of Judah for herself? Who alone of the royal seed was saved? How? Observe who anointed Joash and probably served as the real ruler until Joash grew to maturity. Observe the death of Athaliah. Note also the place of the Mosaic covenant in the mind of Jehoiada. How is Joash's reign described? Note the continued threat of Syria.

TUESDAY

Read chapters 13 and 14. How is Jehoahaz' reign in Israel described? Note his trouble with Hazael the king of Syria. Observe the story of the power of the bones of Elisha after his death. Note the reference again to the Mosaic covenant. What is told about Amaziah and Uzziah? Observe the expansion program of Jeroboam II and the description of his character. He lived in a period when Assyria was threatening Syria, and Syria was afraid to move toward Israel.

WEDNESDAY

Read Amos 1-2; 4:1-5; 5:10-24; 6:4-8. Note the dating of Amos in 1:1 and the geographic pattern in 1:2—2:5. What sins of Israel are underscored in chapter 2? What does Amos say to the women in 4:1-3? How does 5:10-24 move toward the grand climax of verse 24? Compare 6:4-8 with 4:1-3. Summarize your impressions of Amos.

THURSDAY

Read Hosea 1-3; 4; 11; 14:1-7. Note the period designated in 1:1, the family relationships which are involved in chapters 1-3, and the redemptive love in the repurchase of Hosea's wife. Observe also the sins condemned in chapter 4, the love expressed in chapter 11, and the strong appeal of chapter 14.

FRIDAY

Read 2 Kings 15 and 16. How is the reign of Azariah (Uzziah) summarized? Compare 2 Chronicles 26. Jotham became co-regent. Note the series of kings in 15:8-31 and the summary of the reign of each. Pul of 15:19 is Tiglath-pileser III. Note that only one of the last five kings inherited the throne. Study the reigns of Jotham and Ahaz carefully, noting the gradual encroachment and the final acceptance of Assyrian worship by Ahaz. Compare 2 Chronicles 28. The moral fall of Israel is now clear.

SATURDAY

Read Isaiah 1; 7:1-17; 9:6-9; and 10:5-11. Observe that Isaiah, while speaking also to Israel, is dated with reference to Judah. What challenges are given in chapter 1? How did Isaiah encourage Ahaz to demonstrate faith in chapter 7? Note the sign Isaiah proposes and the context in which it occurs. To Ahaz there was probably no reference to Christ, but in Matthew 1:23 this is indicated. Observe the characteristics of the new king promised in 9:6-9 and the fulfillment in Christ. What view of wicked kings in history is presented in 10:5-11?

SUNDAY

Read 2 Kings 17; Micah 1:1; 2:1-5; 3:1-12; 4:1-7; 5:1-4; 6:8. How did Hoshea lead to the fall of Jerusalem? Shalmaneser V (727-722 b.c.) was succeeded by Sargon II (722-705) just before Samaria fell in 721 b.c. Sargon's claim to have captured 27, 290 prisoners and to have deported them may be exaggerated (see James B. Pritchard, *Ancient Near Eastern Texts,* p. 284).

Note in Micah the period indicated for his prophecy, the similarity of 2:1-5 to Amos, the challenge to the leaders in chapter 3, the promises of chapter 4, the message of 5:1-4, and the use of this passage in Matthew 2:6. How is Micah's message summarized in 6:8? What elements of Amos and Hosea are summarized here? Micah combined social justice and redemptive mercy.

DETAILED STUDY

In this study we propose to recognize the rise and fall of Israel, the threat to Judah, and the message of the prophets to the people of their day.

A. THE RISE OF ISRAEL. Chs. 13-14.

It will be helpful to review the list of kings given in the chart on page 114 above. Jehoahaz (815-801), Joash (801-786), and Jeroboam II (786-746) mark the rise of Israel to new prominence, especially the two latter kings.

1. In order to understand this period, we must recognize the fact that Adad-nirari III, who reigned in Assyria from 811 to 783 b.c., broke the back of Damascus, the capital of Syria, and made Ben-hadad II, son and successor to Hazael, a tribute-paying vassal king. His power was likewise extended to Tyre, Sidon, Edom, and Philistia. Weakened by internal problems and having ineffectual rulers as his successors, the kingdom of

Assyria was unable to extend its grip to Israel and Judah until the accession of Tiglath-pileser in 745 B.C. Egypt was not a threat in this period. Therefore the period from 801-746 B.C. was a time when these large nations were not putting pressure on Israel or Judah. Details will be found in the sources suggested for additional reading.

2. Examine the reference to Hazael and the changing fortunes of Israel in 13:1-9. Observe that the Lord delivered Israel from Hazael and Ben-hadad. The Assyrian king may have been the savior sent by God.

3. Note especially in 13:22-25 the threat of Hazael of Syria, the deliverance by the God of the covenant, and the fact that Joash defeated Hazael (or Ben-hadad) three times and recovered the cities of Israel. This repeats the idea of expansion through a weakened Syria.

4. Read 14:8-14 for the challenge to war by Amaziah, king of Judah, after he had succeeded against the Edomites in the south. The consequence of his stubbornness, as we have seen, was the making of Judah a vassal state to Israel for a time. Israel was expanding both northward and southward.

5. Observe the brief account of the reign of Jeroboam II in 14:23-29. Note the expansion of Israel during his reign. "The entrance of Hamath as far as the sea of the Arabah" is well into the territory ordinarily claimed by Syria. Note that Jeroboam is referred to as one through whom God saved Israel, even though he was an evil man. Observe the further reference to Hamath and Damascus in verse 28. The text of this verse is obscure, but it suggests expansion of Israel. Every indication in extracanonical sources is that Jeroboam II was a very successful king who extended the borders of Israel as far as they had been extended under Solomon. His building program in Samaria, his holding back of the Moabites and the Ammonites, and his increase in trade were all marks of his reign. However, as Amos so clearly shows, the nation was suffering from internal moral and spiritual weakness. Let us lift out a few of the major indictments of Amos against the established order in Israel.

B. The Message of Amos.

We have already suggested the reading of certain key passages in Amos. Let us examine these a little more closely.

1. Re-examine 2:6-8 for specific charges made by Amos. Note the apparent legality of selling the righteous for silver, as Jezebel got rid of Naboth in an apparently legal manner by having false charges brought against him. Observe also the reference to trampling the poor in the dust. Note also the adultery practiced, perhaps at the shrines of false worship. Compare 8:4-6 for further details.

2. In 4:1-5, observe the description of the wicked women of Samaria, who oppress the poor and insist that their husbands bring them wine to drink. Observe also in verses 4 and 5 the empty worship at Bethel and at Gilgal, which stems from the desire of the people and not from the command of God.

3. In this same vein, note further details in 6:4-7 concerning the rich people in Samaria. Their lolling luxury, their gluttony, their effort at self-entertainment, and their drunkenness make them anything but people well-pleasing to God. They do not seem to realize that their nation is decaying from within and stands on the brink of ruin.

4. Chapter 5 underscores once again the necessity of bringing conduct and worship into line with the whole will of God. "Seek good, and not evil, that you may live," Amos commands. After warning those who desire the day of the Lord, Amos says they will find it a day of certain judgment. Verse 24 serves as a summary of the message of Amos. It is as pertinent today as in the time of Jeroboam II.

C. The Message of Hosea.

Again we must lift out a few samples of Hosea's message. He probably began his prophetic work soon after Amos, perhaps near the end of the reign of Jeroboam II.

1. We have already noted the personal experience indicated in chapters 1-3. Imagine the heartbreak of having his wife forsake him and his children and going to a life of immorality,

if not of sacred prostitution! Now note especially 2:14-23, which is a promise of the way God will win back his unfaithful covenant people. Thus the experience of Hosea with his errant wife is parallel to God's experience with His unfaithful people. Out of this understanding, and out of his deeper insight concerning the redemptive love of God, Hosea bought back his wife and sought to help her live faithfully.

2. Let us lift out a few thrusts in chapters 4 and 5. For instance, note the charge to the people in 4:1-3. Unfaithfulness to God, swearing, lying, killing, stealing, committing adultery, all come under the prophet's denunciation. In this same chapter, verses 11-19 give a description of false worship, of harlotry, of drunkenness, without parallel in the prophetic writings.

3. The warnings to the leaders may also be noted. How telling the indictment of the priests and prophets in 4:4-10! They have failed to teach fidelity, having rejected the knowledge of God themselves. They are both greedy and unfaithful. The political leaders are likewise warned in 5:1-2 and especially in 5:13-14, where clever politics have been attempted as a cure for the moral ills of an unfaithful people.

4. Yet Hosea underscores the love of God for His unfaithful people. For instance, we have noted the figure of the father-child relationship in chapter 11. Observe the picture of a father teaching a child to walk, holding it in his arms. Observe also the heartbreak of a father who finds it so hard to give up His people. Like the "husband" whose unfaithful wife has broken his heart, now Israel is as a child who forsakes the love of a father. It is in this vein that chapter 14 makes an appeal for Israel to return to the God of love who will heal Israel's unfaithfulness, and who will re-establish His covenant people in prosperity and faithfulness.

Thus Amos and Hosea denounce the weakness of their society. Amos calls for social justice in human relations, and Hosea emphasizes the love of God for His covenant people. Yet love goes unrequited in the days of Israel's apparent success. And does not Israel become a picture of the United States? Is our nation morally sick even in its time of prosperity? What would God say to us today? Do we dare to listen? And to obey?

D. The Survival of Judah. Chs. 11-14.

Now let us go back to pick up the success story of Judah. It is less impressive than that of Israel.

1. Chapter 11 records the effort of Athaliah, the daughter of Ahab and Jezebel, and the wife of Jehoram, king of Judah, to wipe out the seed royal and to take the kingdom for herself. Who alone was saved? We have observed that Jehoiada the priest brought about the anointing and recognition of Joash (Jehoash) as king when he was seven years old, and overthrew Athaliah. We have also observed that Jehoiada then renewed the loyalty of the people to their king, and also renewed the Sinai covenant between God and His people (see verses 17-20). Let us also observe the religious reforms that followed the destruction of the Baal priest and the tearing down of the altars for the worship of Baal. Athaliah had brought the worship of Baal-Melkart into Judah as her mother Jezebel had done in Israel, but probably in less widespread fashion. The anointing of Joash was therefore a part of a religious reform in Judah.

2. We have already recognized the reform movement carried forward under Jehoash. Let us note again the relations of the king of Judah with the king of Syria. In 2 Kings 12:17-18 we are told that Jehoash took the gifts from the Temple to buy off Hazael, king of Syria. Second Chronicles 24:17-27 gives further details about Jehoash's false worship after the death of Jehoiada, and his final death at the hands of his servants after he had been wounded by the Syrians. The efforts of Jehoash to extend the borders of Judah were not so successful.

3. The success of Amaziah in extending the borders of Judah against the Edomites is reported in 14:7; it is given in much greater detail in 2 Chronicles 25. His foolish challenge to the king of Israel and the consequent looting of the Temple and making Judah a vassal state to Israel have been observed. Little is said about Azariah (Uzziah) in 2 Kings 14 and 15 beyond the usual formula. However, in 2 Chronicles 26 we learn of his

leprosy after he became proud and of the fact that he had extended the borders of Judah into Philistia as Amaziah had done in Edom. Jotham his son became coregent after his father became a leper and sought to maintain an expanded Judah.

4. The struggle for survival became more marked in the reign of Ahaz. Observe the reported sacrifice of his son by Ahaz in 2 Kings 16:2-4. You may recall a similar sacrifice by the king of Moab in a time of crisis (2 Kings 3:27). Observe the crisis in which Ahaz found himself (16:5-9). The Edomites were moving in from the south and Syria-Israel from the north. What request did he make of Tiglath-pileser of Assyria? What bribe did he offer for this help? His request was like asking for protection from Russia. Even though this move provided immediate relief, it would cost his nation dearly in the end. Isaiah 7:1— 8:8 should be read in this connection. Isaiah counseled trust in God, and predicted that Rezin of Syria and Pekah of Israel would soon be routed, as indeed they were. Assyria under Tiglath-pileser III was already on the move. But Ahaz refused either a sign from God or to wait for God. His bad bargain and his idolatrous worship, imported from Assyria as a vassal king, both proved serious blows to the future of Judah. Whether Ahaz or Hezekiah weathered the fall of Samaria becomes a matter of correct chronology. *The Westminster Historical Atlas,* p. 15, gives Ahaz' dates as 735-715 B.C., and this would make Ahaz the king of Judah during the fall of Samaria in 722/721 B.C. This problem will be treated briefly in the next lesson.

The political picture in Judah therefore moves from near extinction of the Davidic line under Athaliah to a partial expansion under Amaziah and Azariah, to near destruction under Ahaz, who brought Judah into subjection to Assyria. The reign of Ahaz popularized Assyrian worship in the Temple area and had serious results in later history.

E. THE FALL OF ISRAEL.

Of the last five kings of Israel, only one succeeded his father, and he reigned for only two years. The other four took the throne by murdering their predecessor. This is an illustration of the period of anarchy which preceded the actual fall of Israel. However, there was an external threat as well as internal weakness in Israel during this period. Tiglath-pileser III (745-727 b.c.) aimed at building a great empire, not merely at taxing neighboring peoples. His extension of his reign over Babylonia is not our major concern. We are concerned with his movements westward toward Palestine and Egypt. It appears that Azariah (Uzziah), even though he was leprous, was an organizer of a coalition against Assyrian aggression late in his reign (about 743 b.c.). This is reported in John Bright, *A History of Israel,* pp. 252-253, and in James B. Pritchard, *Ancient Near Eastern Texts,* pp. 282 ff. By not later than 738 b.c., Israel was one of the areas under Assyrian domination. Matters went from bad to worse in Israel.

1. Observe in 15:8-12 the short reign of Zechariah, the son of Jeroboam II. How was he killed? With what result?

2. For how long did Shallum reign? Note how the reign of Menahem is described in 15:14-22. Observe his ruthlessness against those who did not support him. Observe two other important features of his reign. How much did he pay to Tiglath-pileser (Pul)? Where did he get the money? Think of the effect of this exaction each year.

3. Pekahiah had the distinction of inheriting the throne from his father. Note the description of his reign and his death at the hands of Pekah in 15:23-26.

4. How is Pekah's reign described in verses 27-29? If you will check the places mentioned on a map, you will find that Tiglath-pileser cut off the whole northern region of Israel, and carried the people captive. The region around Samaria was left. Observe how Pekah's policy described in 15:29—16:9 resulted in the capture of Damascus of Syria. The invasion of 733 b.c., not reported here, was a devastating blow to Israel's hopes of independence.

5. According to chapter 17, with whom did Hoshea conspire against Shalmaneser V (727-722 b.c.)? With what result? The attack of Shalmaneser against the conspirators in 724 b.c. led

to the capture of Hoshea and the siege and fall of Samaria after two years. This came early in 721 B.C., just a short time after Sargon II had succeeded his father as king of Assyria. We have noted the report of 27,290 captives from Samaria, which may be an Assyrian king's exaggeration. Whether correct or not, Samaria fell and the Northern Kingdom was no more. A mixed population remained to write the history of the Samaritans in later times.

6. The remainder of chapter 17 attributes the fall of Israel and the danger to Judah to unfaithfulness to the covenant relation between God and His people. It underscores the refusal to hear the message of the prophets. To two others of these we again turn our attention.

F. The Message of Isaiah and Micah.

In Isaiah 1-39 and in Micah we have the prophetic picture of conditions in Israel and Judah during the period of crisis centering in and extending beyond 721 B.C. We cannot deal with the message of these prophets in detail, but would like to lift out a few emphases.

1. Examine Isaiah 1 again for the description of the moral and spiritual sickness of the people. Observe how this compares with the message of Amos delivered earlier to Israel. Compare Isaiah 5:8-23 and the series of woes pronounced there. Examine also 10:1-4 for a similar analysis of the sins of Judah.

2. Observe Isaiah 10:5-11 carefully. Note that the Assyrians plunder and destroy other nations freely of their own will. Yet Isaiah sees Assyria as the rod of God's anger. Assyria does not mean to be so. Assyria acts freely from her own greed. But the sovereign God of the nations is the Lord of history. Chapters 13-23 provide a good commentary on this view.

3. Observe in Isaiah 9:2-7 and 14:1-7 the promise of a new kind of messianic leadership and the promise of the restoration of the remnant of Judah. Both of these ideas are characteristic of Isaiah. Although he was fully aware of the problems of Israel, Isaiah addressed himself primarily to Judah.

4. We have already examined some key passages in Micah, which are addressed to Samaria and Jerusalem (1:1). Observe the sins described in 2:1-5, and the similarity of Micah's message to that of Amos and Hosea in this respect. Observe also his indictment of the political and religious leaders in 3:1-12. They devise wickedness on their beds, covet fields and seize them as Jezebel took Naboth's vineyard for Ahab, take away a man and his house, and many other such things which arouse the fierce anger of the Lord. They also try to hush the prophet who calls them to task, and would silence even the Spirit of God.

5. Micah 4:1-7 points to the return of the remnant. This may be compared with Isaiah 14:1-7. Observe how Micah 5:2-4 is related to Isaiah 9:2-6. The character of God pictured in Micah 7:18-20 may be noted in this connection. The summary of Micah's message in 6:8 brings Amos, Hosea, and Micah together. They spoke of justice and mercy and obedience to God. They still speak of the same things to us.

    The fall of Israel was a spiritual as well as a political tragedy. Israel lost her sense of mission under God. She no longer had a reason for living. Both 2 Kings 17 and the message of the prophets bear eloquent testimony to her moral fall. What is our mission? Has our nation lost its soul and its reason for being? Have we as individuals and as a church come to the point where we would save ourselves as a good thing in itself? Let us learn from history! Let our eyes be fixed not on our survival but on our service, not on our traditions but on the whole will of God, not on our purposes but on the mission of a child of God and a nation under God.

G. Lessons in Living.

1. Each student must draw his own conclusions from his study. These are always more important than those suggested by anyone else. The Spirit of God speaks to each person with an open and seeking mind. Make your own list of lessons in living. To this list we would add:

2. The importance of faithfulness in worship. Whether in the message of the prophets or in the experience of Israel and

Judah, this stands out boldly. Character and conduct grow out of genuine worship of the one true God.

3. The significance of keeping conduct in harmony with worship. True worship must express itself in right conduct before God. No individual, no king, no princes, no school of prophets, and no family of priests can make their own rules of conduct. These are revealed by God and cannot be changed at will. For the covenant people they are part and parcel of faithfulness to God.

4. The effect of worship on political life. To be sure, Israel and Judah were bound up with other nations and with the larger nations. However, both Judah and Israel indulged in weaknesses which beclouded the thinking of those who made national policy. The series of usurpations of the throne in Israel and the failure of nerve on the part of Ahaz of Judah serve as illustrations.

5. The sovereignty of God over the nations. God is Lord of history even though He does not ordinarily intervene directly in history. He works through moral principles that weaken or strengthen the nations. His purpose is the key to history.

SUGGESTIONS FOR FURTHER READING

A. COMMENTARIES:

Barnes, W. E., *The Second Book of the Kings* (Cambridge Bible), pp. 53-94.

Dentan, Robert C., *I and II Kings, I and II Chronicles* (Layman's Bible Commentary, Vol. 7).

The Interpreter's Bible, Vol. 3, pp. 244-286.

Montgomery, J. A., *A Critical and Exegetical Commentary on the Books of Kings* (I.C.C.), pp. 416-480.

Skinner, John, *Kings* (The New Century Bible), pp. 335-382.

B. INTRODUCTORY AND BACKGROUND MATERIAL:

Anderson, Bernhard W., *Understanding the Old Testament,* pp. 222-275.

Bright, John, *A History of Israel,* pp. 234-261.

    The Kingdom of God, pp. 57-78.

Finegan, Jack, *Light from the Ancient Past,* revised edition, pp. 184-190, 206-210.

Napier, B. Davie, *Song of the Vineyard,* pp. 199-229.

Pritchard, James B., *Archaeology and the Old Testament,* pp. 134-153.

Wright, G. Ernest, *Biblical Archaeology*, pp. 160-163; abridged edition, pp. 102-107.

Young, Edward J., *An Introduction to the Old Testament*, pp. 200-209.

QUESTIONS FOR THOUGHT AND DISCUSSION

1. If you were speaking as a prophet, what sins of America would you decry? Why these? How would you illustrate? Try paraphrasing key passages in the prophets we have noted.
2. How can you as individuals and as a group of dedicated Christains make a difference in the life of your community? Your nation? Your church? Your home?
3. How would you compare the conditions in the United States and the present world with those studied in 2 Kings? What does 2 Kings say to us?
4. Do you think the United States will ever become a subject nation? Why or why not? How much truth is there in the repeated statements of the communists that we are a decadent nation? How do we differ from Italy, France, Great Britain?
5. What injustices in society are we called upon to work at right now? Why these?
6. How can we help others to grasp the message of 2 Kings?

The Fall of Jerusalem and the Captivity of Judah

The last days of Judah may be described as the period of Assyrian decline and Babylonia's ruthless rise to power, of Egypt's decisive defeat and Judah's tragic fall. This was the period of Jeremiah, from 627-586 B.C. The seeds of decay, as Isaiah 1-39 and Micah so clearly teach, were in Judah at the time of Israel's fall in 721 B.C. Assyria ruled with an iron fist from 721 B. C. to the rebellion of Nabopolasser in 626 B.C., but not without previous uprisings from time to time, nor without the necessity of making invasions of Palestine and the west. Details of this period are given in John Bright, *A History of Israel,* pp. 261-271, 282-310. As we shall see, Hezekiah and his successors had to fight for their existence against tremendous odds.

A very real problem in chronology faces us in chapter 18. If 18:13 refers to the invasion of Sennacherib in 701 B.C., which apparently it does, this would place the beginning of Hezekiah's reign in 715 B.C., fourteen years earlier. However, such dating throws the references in 18:1 and 18:9 out of line. W. F. Albright and others date the beginning of Hezekiah's reign at 715 B.C., which allows Ahaz about twenty-one years rather than sixteen. (See Bright, *A History of Israel,* p. 259 and footnote.) Oesterley and Robinson, in an earlier work, place the accession of Hezekiah in 725 B.C. (*A History of Israel,* Vol. I, p. 459).

One view is that the dates in 18:1, 9 are correct and that 18:13 is in error if it is intended to refer to the invasion of Sennacherib in 701 B.C. Sennacherib succeeded Sargon II in 705 B.C., so the fourteenth year after 725 would be 711 B.C. Sargon, not Sennacherib, came to

Ashdod in that year. The other view is that the date of 18:13 is correct, but that the dating of 18:1 and 18:9 does not harmonize. We shall follow the text in its message, favoring a later date for the accession of Hezekiah. Let us now examine 2 Kings, keeping in mind the historical background of these chapters.

DAILY BIBLE READINGS

MONDAY

Read chapters 18 and 19; compare 2 Chronicles 32:1-23 and Isaiah 36 and 37. Observe the summary of Hezekiah's reign in verses 1-12. Note the record of the invasion of Judah by Sennacherib. The Taylor Cylinder containing Sennacherib's account of this invasion says that he took over 200,000 captives, much cattle and beasts, 800 talents of silver and 300 talents of gold (about $2,500,000). The text of 2 Kings 18:14 has 300 talents of silver and 30 talents of gold. Hezekiah had to deplete his resources and tear the gold off the Temple doors to pay the requirement. Work through the remainder of chapters 18 and 19 in terms of the dramatic situation, the conversations, the message of Isaiah, and the result.

You will find other details in 2 Chronicles 32:1-19 and in Isaiah 36. John Bright believes that 18:13—19:37 contains an account of two campaigns, the first reported in 2 Kings 18:13-16 and in Sennacherib's account of his campaign in 701 B.C.; and the remainder of 18:17—19:37 reports another campaign, about 688 B.C., when Tirhakah would have been twenty or more years of age and would have been able to lead an army against Sennacherib (*A History of Israel,* pp. 282-287).

TUESDAY

Read chapters 20 and 21; compare Isaiah 38, 39; 2 Chronicles 33. The time for chapter 20 may be about 703 B.C. Observe the message of Isaiah to Hezekiah, Hezekiah's prayer, the promise made to him, and the cure of the boil. Note the added material in Isaiah 38, especially the song in 38:9-20. Note the sign given to Hezekiah that he would be healed. Compare Isaiah 39 with this story in 2 Kings. Study the description of Manasseh's wicked reign, his idolatry, and his reversal of policy concerning worship in Judah.

Compare 2 Chronicles 33 for further light on Manasseh and Amon.

WEDNESDAY

Read 2 Kings 22 and 23; compare 2 Chronicles 34 and 35. Note the character of Josiah and the stages of his reforms. The book of the Law discovered was probably Deuteronomy 6-26. What did Josiah do when he found this inspired writing calling the people back to the Mosaic covenant? How did he change the worship which had degenerated under Manasseh? Note who placed Jehoahaz on the throne, and who placed Jehoiakim, the oldest son of Josiah, on the throne as a vassal king. How is the reign of these kings described?

THURSDAY

Read Zephaniah 1:1-6; 3:1-7; Nahum 1:1-14; 3:1-7; Habakkuk 1 and 2. Zephaniah spoke most likely between 621 and 612 B.C. Observe his message of judgment against Judah and the leaders in Jerusalem. Nahum is addressed to Nineveh, probably shortly before the fall of Nineveh to the Babylonians and the Medes in 612 B.C. Observe in his message the coming judgment on Nineveh, and the dramatic way in which this judgment of God is described. Habakkuk 1 and 2 are most certainly to be dated either in 609 B.C. or in 605-604 B.C. Observe the problem of chapter 1 and God's answer in chapter 2. Think through the message of these prophets at this period in Judah's history.

FRIDAY

Read 2 Kings 24 and 25; compare 2 Chronicles 36. Within two years after Nebuchadnezzar defeated Egypt decisively at Carchemish, Jehoiakim found himself subject to Babylonia. Three years later he rebelled, and Nebuchadnezzar came to subdue Judah in 598 B.C. It appears that Jehoiakim died just before he arrived, and that Jehoiachin and the best of the people were carried captive to Babylonia. Note in 2 Kings 24, 25, the description of these events and the numbers taken to captivity in 598 B.C. and the later period in 587 B.C. at the fall of Jerusalem. Observe the turn in Jehoiachin's fortune as reported in verses 27-30.

SATURDAY

Read Jeremiah 2:4-13; 4:1-4; 7:1-15; 28:1-17; 31:31-34. Observe the appeal to the covenant and the promise of chapters 2 and 4. This is a part of the early preaching of Jeremiah, 626-621 B.C. Chapter 7 may be associated with the crisis of 605 B.C., when the Babylonians defeated the Egyptians and threatened Judah. Chapter 26 in Jeremiah is a parallel to chapter 7. Note how these chapters explode the false trust in the Temple. Chapter 28 is dated in 594 B.C., four years after the first captivity in 598 B.C. Note the two points of view concerning an early return of these captives. What further word comes in 31:31-34, written or spoken before or soon after the fall of Jerusalem in 587 B.C.? This covenant found greater meaning in Christ.

SUNDAY

Read Ezekiel 3:4-21; 22:1-16; 36:16-28. Ezekiel was among the captives of 598 B.C., and began to speak about 593 B.C. Ezekiel 1-24 is directed primarily to Judah. How is Ezekiel's call described in chapters 1-3? What was Ezekiel's message to Judah in chapter 22? Compare with that of other prophets. Ezekiel 36:16-28, addressed to the exiles in Babylon, tells why the people of Judah were taken captive and promises a new heart as well as restoration. How are these promises expressed? John 3 and Galatians 6:16 probably come from these verses. What have you learned from your daily Bible readings for life today?

DETAILED STUDY

The story in 2 Kings 18-25 tells us very little about the world movements in which the last days of Judah were spent, even though it does report invasions by Sennacherib and Nebuchadnezzar. Details of these movements are given in Bernhard W. Anderson's *Understanding the Old Testament*, pp. 288-356, and in John Bright's *A History of Israel*, pp. 261-319. We will attempt here to give a brief outline placing these chapters in their larger context. In addition, we propose to place the covenant idea in its proper context, especially to show the relation of the Sinai covenant to the Davidic covenant.

A. THE CONTEXT OF CHAPTERS 18-25.

At the time of the fall of Samaria and the final captivity of Israel in 721 B.C., the consequences of Ahaz' appeal to Tiglath-pileser against Hazael of Syria and Pekah of Israel were not all apparent. By becoming subject to Assyria, Ahaz probably prevented Judah from rebelling with Israel in 724 B.C. and from being carried captive with Israel. This was a good thing for Judah. However, the tendency of Ahaz to bring Assyrian and Canaanitish worship into Judah as a national policy cannot be cited as good. The reforms under Hezekiah came while Assyria was busy with Babylonia and other nations. They might not have been possible otherwise.

1. Notice again 18:1-8 as an evidence of Hezekiah's growing independence of Assyria. It will be remembered that it is almost impossible to harmonize all of the references to time in chapter 18. Before recognizing the background of the story of Sennacherib, let us examine 20:12-19.

2. As you read 20:12-19 again and keep Isaiah 39 in mind, you will understand the international aspect of the visit of the envoy from Merodach-baladan of Babylonia. In Assyria, Sargon II had been killed in battle in 705 B.C., and was succeeded by his weaker son Sennacherib. This occasioned plots of revolt, not only in Babylonia, but also in the west. In fact, Babylonia in the east had more promise of success against Assyria if she could stir up trouble in the west. About 703 B.C. the envoys of Babylonia came to visit Hezekiah. It is likely that Hezekiah, against the advice of Isaiah (Isaiah 30:1-7; 31:1-3), made a league with Egypt and with other nations in the west. Hezekiah also busied himself with defenses against Sennacherib (2 Chronicles 32:3-5, 30; 2 Kings 20:20). According to Sennacherib's annals, Padi, the king of Ekron, refused to join the conspiracy and was held prisoner by Hezekiah in Jerusalem. This was the situation when Sennacherib invaded the west in 701 B. C., as reported in 18:13—19:37, with parallels in 2 Chronicles 32:1-21 and Isaiah 36-37. In 18:14-16 we are told that Hezekiah sent to Sennacherib at Lachish and sued for terms. Bernhard W. Anderson treats the whole of 18:13—19: 37 as a continued story of one invasion, but John Bright, as we have already suggested, treats 18:13-16 as one campaign and

18:17—19:37 as another. The major reason appears to be that a reference is made to Tirhakah of Ethiopia in 19:9, and he assumed power in Egypt about 690/689 B.C. Bright assumes a second rebellion by Hezekiah at this time, with Sennacherib coming again to the west in 688 B.C., believing that 18:17—19:37 and Isaiah 36 best fit this context. Whether this is a combined account or not, Sennacherib describes the way in which he took forty-six cities in Palestine and shut Hezekiah up "like a bird in a cage" (James B. Pritchard, *Ancient Near Eastern Texts*, pp. 287-288). This means that Judah increasingly was coming under the domination of Assyria, but struggling to maintain her freedom.

3. Following the death of Hezekiah in 687 B.C., Manasseh came to the throne, reversing his father's policies. Second Kings 21:1 tells us he reigned for 55 years in Jerusalem, but the date of his death is usually placed at 642 B.C. During that time there was a stabilization of power over Babylonia and there were repeated invasions of Egypt by Esar-haddon (681-669), the son and successor to Sennacherib. The domination of Assyria over Egypt continued throughout Manasseh's lifetime. Manasseh remained a vassal to Assyria, both politically and religiously. He paid homage to the Assyrian gods and brought the worship of the astral deities of Assyria into the Temple in Jerusalem. He also restored local pagan shrines, permitting or encouraging the local and foreign fertility cults to be developed. Divination and magic were also made popular. All of this is described in 2 Kings 21. The estimate given of Manasseh in 2 Kings 21, from the point of view of monotheisitic faith as opposed to polytheism, is probably well justified. He did for Judah what Ahab and Jezebel had done for Israel. The sins of Manasseh remained after his death and succession by Amon, and were only partially removed by his vigorous grandson reformer, Josiah (640-609 B.C.).

4. The reign of Josiah and the reforms instituted by him as described in 2 Kings 22-23 (2 Chronicles 34-35) were possible because the Assyrians, after the vigorous fighting of Asshurbanapal against the Medes, the Cimmerians, the Scythians, and

the Babylonians, went into a decline as a world power. In 626 B.C. Nabopolasser of Babylon asserted himself as an independent king. The Medes likewise reasserted themselves under Cyaxeres (625-585 B.C.), and together they set about to dismember the Assyrian Empire. In 614 B.C. Cyaxeres captured Asshur, and in 612 he and Nabopolasser took Nineveh. In 610 they drove the refugee Assyrian government out of Haran. Once again the weakening of an overlord permitted a reform movement to succeed in Judah. We will observe other features of this reform later.

5. A series of tragic events followed the death of Josiah in 609 B.C. It is not clear whether he acted independently or as an ally of Babylonia when he went out to stop Pharaoh Neco of Egypt, who was on his way to assist the fading Assyrians against Nabopolasser at Haran. He probably acted as an ally of Babylonia. The selection of his second son, Jehoahaz, as king by the elders of Judah was only a temporary measure. The Egyptian king three months later returned to Jerusalem, bound Jehoahaz in chains to take to Egypt, and put Josiah's oldest son, Jehoiakim, on the throne as a vassal king. The decisive defeat of Neco by Nebuchadnezzar of Babylon at Carchemish in 605 B.C. once again changed the picture for Judah. Nebuchadnezzar received word of his father's death as he was chasing the Egyptians to their homeland. He secured his throne in Babylon and returned in 603 B.C. to bring Egypt and Palestine under his immediate control. Jehoiakim became a vassal king then to Babylonia instead of Egypt. This is the background against which 24:1-7 should be read. Jehoiakim probably rebelled late in 601 B.C. Nebuchadnezzar sent bands against him, as 24:2 suggests, until he could march against Jerusalem in December, 598 B.C. As we have already suggested, Jehoiakim died about this time and was succeeded by his son Jehoiachin. Read 24:8-17 in this connection. Three months after he began to reign, Nebuchadnezzar captured Jehoiachin and the best of the people of Judah. He carried them to Babylonian captivity. Note the figure of 10,000 captives in 24:14, and a total of 8,000 in 24:16. According to Jeremiah 52:28, 3,023 captives were carried away at this

time. Either the two authors used different sources, or Jeremiah reports only the adult males. Ezekiel was among these captives, as were Jehoiachin and his mother.

6. The reign of Zedekiah was one of rebellion. Probably in 594 B.C., the plot reported and warned against in Jeremiah 27, with the further message in chapter 28 the same year, suggests a spirit of unrest and rebellion in the west. The hope that Jehoiachin and the captives would return, bringing back the vessels of the Temple, was a false hope encouraged by the false prophets. Apparently some advocated a united effort against Babylon to rescue the captives. The final rebellion came in 589, with the Babylonian army coming in 588 to destroy not only other towns, such as Azekah and Lachish (as the Lachish Letters suggest), but to set the siege and to bring about the fall of Jerusalem in 587 B.C. This is described in 2 Kings 24:18—25: 26 and in certain chapters of Jeremiah. The postscript in Jeremiah 40-44 completes the story of the fall of Jerusalem in the biblical accounts. The additional word about Jehoiachin in 2 Kings 25:27-30, dated in 560 B.C., has already been noted.

B. THE COVENANT WITH JUDAH.

The Sinai covenant was designed to be an everlasting covenant with Judah. However, the Davidic covenant bade fair to replace it. Let us see how these covenants are treated.

1. The Davidic Covenant.

In connection with God's refusal to allow David to build the Temple in chapter 7, God promised through the prophet Nathan that David's throne would be established forever (7:8-29). This covenant gained in prominence, and it was in the mind of Solomon in 1 Kings 3:5-14. It may be noted that he was required to obey God's commandments. Just after the dedication of the Temple, in 1 Kings 9:1-9, the covenant promise was renewed with Solomon, again with the condition of obedience, and with the warning that disobedience would bring destruction to his throne and to all Israel. In 1 Kings 15:1-5, the Lord established Abijam in Jerusalem for the sake of David his servant, in spite of Abijam's disobedience. In 2

Kings 21:7-9 another reference is made to the promise to David and Solomon, and to the fact that Manasseh has violated the requirements of the Mosaic covenant. The Davidic covenant required moral obedience, and the Davidic line was subject to the requirements of the Mosaic covenant.

When the last of the Davidic kings was taken captive, it was hoped that Jehoiachin would return. The fact that Zerubbabel was the grandson of Jehoiachin suggests that the Jews expected the Davidic line to rule after the return from Exile. The New Testament interpretation of Jesus as the seed of David (Matthew 1 and Luke 3) and as the spiritual king of God's people of faith carries forward this idea.

2. The Mosaic Covenant.

Prior to the Davidic covenant, the Mosaic covenant was regarded as basic to the life of Israel. For a time after David, only the prophets seem to be aware of the importance of the Mosaic covenant. A significant change took place when the book of the Law (a major portion of Deuteronomy) was found in the Temple during the reforms of Josiah in 621 B.C. Like the prophets of Isaiah's period, notably Hosea, this book of the Law called Israel to obey the revealed will of God. Jeremiah 2:1—4:4 serves as an example. This covenant survived the captivity because it was based on God's choice of a people whom He purposed to redeem. The new covenant of Jeremiah 31:31-34 and Ezekiel 36:16-36, promising to the purged remnant forgiveness and new life, fulfills the Mosaic covenant at its best and points to the new covenant in Jesus Christ.

C. God's Sovereign Purpose.

The key to the Old Testament, as we have suggested before, is the purpose of the eternal God. This God is Lord of the individual, of the nations of the world, and of the whole of history. His purpose will triumph in the end. The judgment upon Israel, Judah, Assyria, Babylonia, and the other nations is an expression of this purpose. So also is the new covenant of the heart. The promised restoration of God's people is an expression of His purpose. Therefore the destruction of Jerusalem, the captivity of

God's people, and the return of the remnant all find their unity in God's purpose. This purpose finds expression in the Mosaic covenant and in a sense in the Davidic covenant. It is the key to history, to redemption, to the future. It points to the coming of the God-man, Jesus Christ, in whom the redemptive purpose of God finds its fullest expression. We live to find our purpose in His purpose, and to make His purpose the goal of our daily living.

D. LESSONS IN LIVING.

1. The student's own lessons in living are always more important for him than are those suggested here. Make your own list first.

2. The way God works in history stands out in chapters 18-25 with peculiar force. The moral forces of history grind slowly, but they grind exceedingly fine.

3. The tenacity of Judah stands out in the midst of more than a hundred years of intrigue and power politics between Egypt to the south, smaller nations round about, and Assyria-Babylonia to the north and east.

4. The prophets and their place in world affairs, particularly the ministries of Isaiah and Jeremiah, speak to the pertinence of religion in politics.

5. Ezekiel (and to a lesser extent Jeremiah) speaks to the fact that prophecy goes on beyond tragedy. God was very much alive even though Judah went to captivity. Both Jeremiah and Ezekiel stand out in bold relief against the background of their times.

6. The sovereign purpose of God is the key to history, to redemption, and to the future. In this purpose we find our purpose, and in fulfilling it we find our destiny.

SUGGESTIONS FOR FURTHER READING

A. COMMENTARIES:

Barnes, W. E., *The Second Book of the Kings* (Cambridge Bible), pp. 94-148.

Dentan, Robert C., *I and II Kings, I and II Chronicles* (Layman's Bible Commentary, Vol. 7).

The Interpreter's Bible, Vol. 3, pp. 287-338.

Montgomery, J. A., *A Critical and Exegetical Commentary on the Books of Kings* (I.C.C.), pp. 480-569.

Robinson, Gordon, *Historians of Israel* (1), pp. 72-78.

Skinner, John, *Kings* (The New Century Bible), pp. 382-448.

B. INTRODUCTORY AND BACKGROUND MATERIAL:

Anderson, Bernhard W., *Understanding the Old Testament*, pp. 275-356.

Bright, John, *A History of Israel*, pp. 261-319.

       The Kingdom of God, pp. 79-126.

Finegan, Jack, *Light from the Ancient Past*, revised edition, pp. 210-227.

Napier, B. Davie, *Song of the Vineyard*, pp. 230-282.

The Westminster Historical Atlas, revised edition, pp. 55-56.

Wright, G. Ernest, *Biblical Archaeology*, pp. 164-179; abridged edition, pp. 108-127.

Young, Edward J., *An Introduction to the Old Testament*, pp. 211-265.

QUESTIONS FOR THOUGHT AND DISCUSSION

1. These questions will deal with the whole series, not with one book alone. Try to formulate your own questions.

2. Examine the background and the basic milieu of each of these books. For what comparable period in history could we look for a parallel from 1250-587 B.C.? Think in terms of U. S. history.

3. Try to get the basic structure of each book in mind. How is it organized? Which books carry forward the story? How?

4. How would you summarize the message of each of these books? Try presenting the structure and the message in some significant way.

5. Lift out five lessons in living that run through the major portion of these books. Why these? How may they be illustrated from the material in the books themselves?

6. Think through the covenants dealt with in these books. How would you discuss the purpose of God as the key to history, to redemption, and to the future?

Suggestions for Twenty-Six Lessons

After considering several possibilities, we propose that those who use twenty-six sessions devote two to each lesson. We suggest that the daily Bible readings serve as the basis for the first study, and that the detailed study be used for the second. The questions for thought and discussion may be used with either. Look at the contents and you will see the thirteen lessons. By devoting two sessions to each, you will have twenty-six.

Persons who wish to make a more thorough study may do so, but the values of a survey come from surveying rather than from detailed study of every part of the material.

If twenty-six sessions are used, we suggest that the additional resources may be used with either approach, but will probably be more helpful when used in connection with the detailed study or the second approach to each lesson.

Use *Teaching the Historical Books* for a more detailed guide for either thirteen or twenty-six sessions.